changes in government after his fall. All these forces and personalities are held together by a focus upon Lenin and a progressive build-up to the climactic event of the Bolshevik Revolution.

The roles of individuals and groups are made clear; political and ideological differences among the many factions are explored fully; and theories, programs and controversial and dramatic events are explained with admirable precision. One of the great dramas of modern history emerges from this incisive portrait of Lenin the revolutionary, just as Lenin himself emerged from the chaotic events leading up to the Russian Revolution.

LENIN AND THE RUSSIAN REVOLUTION

LENIN

and the Russian Revolution

Harold Shukman

FOUNDED 1838

GPPS

G. P. PUTNAM'S SONS
NEW YORK

To the Memory of my Parents

Preface

This book attempts to set out the main course of the events which broadly constituted the revolutionary situation which existed in Russia during the last twenty years or so of Tsarist rule.

The Tsarist regime failed to cope with the dissidence generated by its own conflicting policies, as well as with that which is present in any society. In particular, it failed to recognise and accommodate the forceful appeal of democratic ideas then spreading among a widening sector of the educated and semi-educated public. An overweening propensity to govern solely through a centralised bureaucracy at a time when modernisation was synonymous with democratisation, confirm that the Russian government was victim of its own habits, lacking the capacity to change.

But hidebound behaviour in face of change was not a monopoly of the Tsarist regime. From the liberals to the Socialist Revolutionaries, and including the Marxists, the Russian opposition movement clung to the idea of revolution, regardless of changes which may have rendered their point of view socially irrelevant.

I have tried to emphasise that the habits of government nourished those of opposition, and vice versa. The failure of the Provisional Government, which replaced the Tsar in March 1917, to acquire the governmental habit, and the persistence of the opposition mentality, expressed most clearly by Lenin, offer one explanation of the confusion and apparent aimlessness of those eight months in the middle of 1917: the government did not yet know how to stop behaving like the opposition and begin being the government. The Bolshevik government avoided this failing, thanks to the authoritarian attitude of its founder to all matters of organisation.

While I have not attempted to write a biography of Lenin, nor a history of the party to which he devoted the greater part of his life and all his energies, I have tried to depict the role he played in that party and the significance of the party and its activities against the general background of change in Russia.

In 1920 Bertrand Russell defined Bolshevism as 'an impatient philosophy, which aims at creating a new world without sufficient preparation in the opinions and feelings of ordinary men and women'. Lenin, a year before he died, advised the party to remove its General Secretary, Stalin, from his post and to replace him with someone 'more patient, more loyal, more considerate and attentive to his comrades'. One of my aims has been to show that the 'impatient philosophy' was rather an attitude of mind than a doctrine, and that impatient leadership was an institution of Bolshevism from its inception, rather than a quirk foisted upon it for thirty years by Stalin.

I wish to thank the Warden and Fellows of St Antony's College, Oxford, for the patient hospitality they have shown me while I have been writing this book, and longer. To my wife I am more than grateful for the help she has given me in preparing the manuscript. It is to her that my book owes its merits, to me its flaws and misconceptions.

Contents

LENIN AND THE RUSSIAN REVOLUTION

Introduction

Russia at the beginning of this century confronted problems which derived essentially from the period of Alexander II's reign. The great reforms of the 1860s and 1870s provided the shape and much of the content that Russia's twentieth-century conflicts would assume. The spirit of emancipation, or expediency, which in 1861 had moved Alexander to free Russia's vast peasant population from bondage, also determined his attitude to educated society, which was recognised as possessing a political potentiality far in excess of its limited size. The thrall of control and censorship which Nicolas I had thrown over the intelligentsia was lifted. Alexander wanted to bring Russia's creative element into fruitful intercourse with the state.

One of his most successful moves in this direction was the creation, in 1864, of the *zemstva*, or local government institutions. These were introduced in response to specific limited political demands of a section of the land-owning gentry. But in the course of their existence they engendered political awareness among an increasingly broad section of both gentry and the new middle class. In the process of managing local technical services, public health, agriculture, education, they brought into being a large number of zemstvo employees, recruited from the educated bourgeoisie, or non-gentry, and now transformed into a classless estate of specialists (the so-called third element), all committed to the progressive role of the zemstvo.

Alexander reformed the law courts, the universities and their administration, and the censorship, all in the direction of greater responsibility invested in society. It was widely accepted that the culmination of these changes would be the institution of representative government. This deduction was shared by all shades of educated opinion, though not all were equally sanguine about the prospect.

The hopes and fears aroused by Alexander II's enlightened policies were dashed by the activities of the revolutionaries, who acted within a separate political framework. While the government pursued its liberal policies, the revolutionaries turned increasingly to terrorism as a means of protest against injustice and deprivation of the masses. In the 1860s society as a whole was relatively unaffected by the government's running battle with the revolutionaries, but by the end of the 1870s it was becoming clear that public opinion was moving towards retrenchment, an end to the tension, and the removal of the threat to stability and further progress. It was well known that the ultimate target of the terrorists was the Tsar himself. Terrorism had hardened the heart of the regime and it was only a matter of time before the effects of this hardening would be felt more widely.

Alexander II sought a solution to the mounting dilemma in a dual policy. On the one hand the government must pursue an intensive course to uproot sedition, while on the other hand it must grant political concessions, if only to draw the teeth of the revolutionary menace. But it was on the very day, 1 March 1881, that he had approved a plan for a representative assembly that the Tsar was assassinated.

The reaction of the new Tsar, Alexander III (1881–1894), to the murder of his father was to clamp down hard on all political expression and independent social activity in all sectors. At the same time he was resolved to try to consolidate and build on the economic foundations for the modernisation and stabilisation of the country, which his father had begun. The political outlook of the Tsar and his closest advisers was contained in their evident belief that the political consciousness of what was already a professional intelligentsia could be submerged in a dynamic economic programme. They were blind to the paradox that such a programme could only produce equally dynamic social changes, and hence new political needs.

The 1880s and 1890s saw the government stimulating economic activity, giving rise to a sudden upsurge of large-scale industry, which dramatically put Russia into the tables of comparison with western European industrial output. Government financial and industrial policies were in essence intensified versions of the policies of the previous reign.

The industrialisation of Russia, and hence the stabilisation of the regime, had been expected to follow upon the emancipation. A vast pool of untied wage labour was created; fresh capital both for reinvestment in modern agriculture and new investment in industry was generated by the compensation paid by the government to landowners for the loss of their serfs. Boosted agricultural output (grain exports tripled by the end of the 1870s) stimulated the building of railways, which in turn created a demand for steel and machinery. By the mid-1870s, with the help of Welsh skills and Russian government capital, an iron and steel industry was flourishing in the Ukraine. Oil production in the Caucasus, first extracted there by Swedes in the 1870s, was greatly facilitated by the completion, a decade later, of the Trans-Caucasian railway, linking the Caspian with the Black Sea.

In the almost total absence of an indigenous Russian capitalist class, these achievements were accomplished with the help of foreign capital, which was also attractive for the industrial know-how associated with it. The Russian government pursued a policy of attracting foreign investment by offering high interest rates, government guarantees, and high import tariffs to create a reassuring atmosphere in the raw conditions.

Simultaneously, the government, bent on containing the social effects of its own programme, conducted a social policy which outstripped that of Nicolas I in its obscurantism and reaction. Rabid chauvinism was fostered to express the unity of the Russian people, who, shocked by the assassination of the Tsar-liberator, were withdrawing into a mood of conservative apolitism. But xenophobia in Russia at that time, as before and after, meant the isolation of a great majority of the intelligentsia, not all of whom were politically engaged, but most of whom derived their spiritual nourishment from western culture.

In education and the universities, a narrow nationalist approach was coupled with a police-like supervision of students' activities. Censorship was intensified again, and in general the police resumed their accustomed role in all areas of public activity. After the assassination a Special Security Department, the *Okhrana*, was set up to deal vigorously with the revolutionaries, which steadily accumulated so detailed and subtle a knowledge of illegal activities, that eventually it would be able to penetrate into the core of any organisation in Russia. The ubiquitousness of the *Okhrana*, however, and its zeal, resulted in an overspill of police activity which in time generated specific social attitudes to authority. First it created an exaggerated and distorted image of the regime itself. Instead of focussing on the economic and social change, which was going on at an extraordinary rate, the attention of the educated population was concentrated on the political immaturity of the regime.

Secondly, a conspiratorial outlook was artificially foisted on even moderate opinion, which had the effect, notably in 1905, of over-polarising political views. Thus a law-abiding political party would be accused by the radicals of collaborating with the government, while constitutionalist politicians to the left of centre were lumped together with the terrorists in the eyes of the right wing and of the monarchy.

Thus the government's policy of trying to divert public interest from politics to economics, as a means of retaining national obedience, produced precisely the opposite effect. And in the economic and social fields, too, the political component was to emerge as paramount.

It was the view of most shades of opinion that the problem of the peasantry constituted a major social issue, demanding the full attention of state and society. The view was no less widely held forty years after 1861, but now it acquired the same political connotation which the terrorists of the 1860s and 1870s had attached to it: it became a vehicle of protest. The emancipation of the serfs in 1861 had not fundamentally altered the legal status of the peasant, nor made his economic function more effective. Although he and his family were no longer the personal property of the landowning gentry, they were instead compulsorily inscribed members of village communes. The commune was responsible as a body for the payment of taxes and for the repayment to the state of the money advanced to serf-owners in exchange for the land granted to the communes in 1861. The communes themselves had powers to control the movements and labours of their members in order to ensure the security of the state's loans, as well as to maintain law and order in the village now that the gentry were deprived of their absolute authority.

The last thing the communes were capable of was economic efficiency. A medieval strip system prevailed, the strips often being scattered and subject to periodic rotation among the households of the commune, thus uprooting any incipient sense of ownership or responsibility. This pleased the agrarian socialists, who interpreted it as the Russian peasant's innate revulsion from property and natural tendency to collectivism. This, however, was a myth, and, apart from the gross inefficiency entailed in the system, what was noticeable by the turn of the century was a growing number of successful peasants who had managed to consolidate their strips, pay off their mortgage, and were on the way to becoming self-sufficient farmers.

The great majority, however, ground out their existence on too little land, with too little money for seeds and equipment, too large families, and a primitive attitude towards agriculture. State taxes were heavier on them than on the gentry, and in the 1890s during the period of Russia's great industrial expansion it was the peasants who bore the brunt of new indirect taxation, which contributed to the government's policy of industrialisation.

Peasant misery, affecting the vast majority of the population, was viewed sourly by the government which saw in it potential, and indeed often actual, outbursts of violence. The much lighter burden on the gentry had been intended to ensure their continuation as the mainstay of the regime in the countryside after 1861. But the gentry had always been an urban-oriented class, accepting their country estates as gratuities for state service, but only in individual cases developing an interest or concern for the problems of land cultivation and village life. Thus a large part of the land payments after 1861, instead of being applied to new equipment and supplies, went on paying for the maintenance of a standard of living better suited to a privileged past.

By 1900 the gentry had borrowed from government funds almost as much as the whole cost of the emancipation, and were taking loans from private banks against grain which had not yet been harvested. The emancipation had left the gentry holding about half of all cultivated land. By 1905 it had fallen to one quarter. Land speculators, successful peasants, go-ahead landowners were waiting to buy. The government's hope that the gentry would remain the chief source of stability was disappointed. To fill the vacuum, which revealed itself in rural disturbances during the early 1880s, the government forced the role of keepers of the peace on to the most 'reliable' of the gentry, to be exercised through the zemstvos. This policy engendered a political divergence within the zemstvo movement between the professionals, whose loyalty was to the zemstvo, and the deputies who now conceived of their role as guiding the zemstvo along lines congenial to government policy.

Poverty, arrears in redemption payment, the certainty that they would never possess the land they tilled, deprived of legal status, and watched like prisoners at worst, children at best—this was the situation of the majority of peasants on the eve of 1905, and any reform of so large a problem had to be radical to be effective. Outright ownership by the peasants of the land they tilled was the basis of all but the most reactionary or the most utopian thought on the subject. The peasant's eternal complaint that he did not own the land he tilled, or that his holding was not economic, was taken up almost as a fetish.

The government's policy of attracting foreign capital for its modernisation schemes was hampered by the fact that the rouble was not on the gold standard and therefore was vulnerable to fluctuations on western markets. With the aim, therefore, of stabilising the currency by the accumulation of gold, the government altered the system of taxation, in the mid-1880s, from direct to indirect, and thus proceeded to draw the major part of revenue from the largest, but also the poorest, section of the population, the peasantry. Revenue rose, and, with the new boom period opening in 1885 in the west, the Russian economy began the growth for which the 1890s earned the name of the 'golden decade'.

The economic policies of Alexander III's reign were taken over at the end of his reign by one of the most dynamic of Russia's ministers, Sergei Witte. From 1892, two years before the accession of Nicolas II, until 1903 Witte held the office of Finance Minister. Trained as a railway administrator, Witte embodied bureaucratic egocentricity. He believed that Russia's problems could be tackled only by an efficient and highly centralised administration, and he cited the reformist tradition of Peter the Great as proof. When the zemstvos attacked his policy as crippling to the over-burdened peasantry, he countered by persuading the Tsar that an enhanced civil service could perform the functions of local self-government more efficiently and less costly than they. Moreover an enlightened bureaucracy would, he claimed, guarantee social progress and individual liberty as important requisites of progressive and prosperous development. His prescription for the functions of the state and society envisaged the fullest and freest expression of social and individual aspirations, safeguarded by an omniscient administration, to which should be left the entire business of government.

These arguments, composed in a memorandum to the Tsar called *Autocracy and the Zemstvo* (1899), while intended to influence Nicolas to make changes in the bureaucracy, were equally important in convincing him that further concessions to public initiative in the sphere of the zemstvos would lead inevitably to greater conflict between state and society and eventually to the demand for a constitution. It was an argument Nicolas had heard many times before, indeed it lay at the root of his father's rule, and it would continue to guide him in all his confrontations with future demands from society. Witte, however, was an opportunist, and when in 1905 it was apparent that both Tsar and administration were in danger of losing their grip, he it was who persuaded Nicolas to cut the autocracy's losses and permit a parliament to be established.

Under Witte's policies Russia leapt into the position of a world industrial power. By 1897 she achieved currency stability and the rouble went on the gold standard. A favourable trade balance was created by high tariffs and boosted exports. The high tariffs attracted foreign capital, stimulated domestic initiative, and thus promoted growth. The tax burden was reduced for productive landowners in order to promote grain export; but taxation on alcohol, sugar and tobacco fell heavily on the peasant population. The government invested all its hope for stability in the industrialisation and relied upon the unproductive peasant for revenue. Witte plainly expected to reach economic dry land before the peasants collapsed.

It was a cardinal deficiency in the government's thinking that, in shifting peasants off the land and into the cities to man the enormous new industrial enterprises, it failed to take into account the social and political implications of its own dynamic economic policy. Industrialisation introduced entirely new elements into Russian life. By 1900 the problems of the landed gentry and the peasantry, which had characterised social tension in the nineteenth century, had been equalled by the problems of a new industrial middle class and an urban proletariat.

The moral bond of nearly mutual dependence that had tied landlord and peasant was absent between employer and worker, where the contract was reduced to a bare exchange of wages for labour. Both classes were highly volatile. The employers as a class were fully committed to further change, and where the peasant had to submit to the needs of the land, and thereby indirectly to the needs of the landlord, the urban worker could not yet identify his own future with that of the enterprise. What Marx called the alienation of the workers from the means of production came to Russia on a large scale and almost in a single phase: the process of martialling the journeymen and ex-peasants under the capitalist factory roof took place in Russia more rapidly than for example in England. In the important and dynamic sector of industry the scale was mammoth, and the rate of growth was commonly designated as 'American'.

It was a feature of early Russian industrialisation that it depended heavily upon foreign investment, and this indeed would remain significant throughout the remainder of the nation's pre-Bolshevik economic life. Private wealth during the first phase of industrialisation under Alexander II came mainly from existing entrepreneurs and factory-owning families or from ex-land-owners and big merchants, but accounted for no more than a quarter of investment at that period. The boom conditions of the 1880s, however, created ideal soil for speculators in trade and commerce, and they arose from every class of the population, though predominantly from the petty bourgeoisie, the *meshchan-stvo* or townsmen—tradesmen, artisans and so on. By the turn of the century a second and third generation had arrived and, with education, assurance and a sense of style, had much in common with the professional middle class, or with their counter-parts in western Europe.

Russia's late entry into the world market had necessitated a measure of protection for her nascent class of industrial capitalists, who thus like the gentry identified their own prospects with those of the government. This sense of dependence was most evident in the initial stages of the industrialisation in the 1880s, when the government's reactionary political outlook was matched by the shocked withdrawal of the public from politics that followed the assassination of Alexander II. But by the turn of the century Russian industrialists had acquired, in addition to great personal and corporate wealth, a sense of economic power grossly out of keeping with their political impotence.

The urban middle classes found little difficulty in acquiring this outlook. With the men of the zemstvos they shared the belief that, although they were bearing vital burdens of the national economy, they were being deprived by the government of any appropriate means of expression. The only points of contact between state and society were in the network of the official administration. The pressing needs of both the agrarian and the industrial sectors, as expressed by the hobbled zemstvos and their limited city counterparts, the town councils (*duma*), became the basis of a general demand for some system of national representation, independent of the bureaucracy, and reflecting Russia's development towards the western European type of industrial society.

In the legal sense there was no class of workers in Russia. Workers were for the most part peasants in new employment, or townspeople, classed as petty-bourgeois. In 1900 over one quarter still retained ties with their old village, either as tax-paying members of the commune to which they had once belonged actively, or, depending on the region, as seasonal labour, or even as smallholders. In the forty years since the emancipation the industrial labour population had grown from under 1,000,000 to over 3,000,000, and, while this figure hardly seemed to count against the total population of 130,000,000, it represented a highly concentrated social force.

The workers' outlook varied considerably according to their national and regional origins. In the Baltic and Polish provinces, for example, where ship-building, textile and metal manufacture had achieved modern standards over several generations, the working population was advanced in comparison with the workers of more recently industrialised provinces. In such advanced centres, after several generations of factory and workshop life, distinctive features had developed which might be typical of any western workers: a pride and tradition in skills, the habit of routine and regular attendance at work, a concern for money but not for property, and eagerness and respect for education, for themselves as much as for their children, a less collective; or communal attitude to life than that of the peasant.

It was in such centres as, for instance, Warsaw, Lodz, St Petersburg, that the first labour protests took place. The great iron, steel and coal centres in the Ukraine, based on Kharkov and Ekaterinoslav (now Dnepropetrovsk), developed massively during the period of Russia's economic upsurge in the last twenty years of the nineteenth century. The workers here were not yet in the main hereditary proletarians, but were the amalgamation of various migrations of peasants and artisans.

Between the two extreme types of factory labour, one the hereditary factory masses of the Baltic and Polish provinces and St Petersburg, the other an almost half-time peasantry, there remained a large sector derived from the lower middle class of townspeople. This middle type of labour remained typical of certain regions, and was not subjected to integration into large scale industry. In the western Ukraine, and in what are now Belorussia and Lithuania, centred on Vilna and Minsk, Kiev and Belostok, the working-class element was represented by small-town traders, small-scale industry, such as match and cigar manufacture, glove-making, brushes and bristles, leather-working and tailoring. The area to which Jews were restricted by law, the Pale of Jewish Settlement, was partly in these areas, where Jews, often a majority of town dwellers, lived in overcrowded poverty.

But a combination of small towns, small workshops, ethnic or religious affinity, and a sense of isolation, often welcome, produced a certain cohesion among these Jewish and Polish workers which made it easier to organise a labour movement in the Pale and in Poland than among the less integrated masses of the Russian industrial cities.

In spite of the varied and uneven development of the Russian working class, some generalisations can nonetheless be made. The comparatively low productivity of the Russian worker was at least one reliable indication that Russian management had not yet learned the best ways to employ its labour. Living conditions may have been marginally better in some places than rural conditions for the poor peasants as a whole; but squalor, or even austerity, tends to create discontent in towns much sooner than worse conditions can produce in the countryside.

To add to the misery that fast industrial growth entailed in an age when the accommodation of labour took second place after the establishment of factories, the attitude of entrepreneurs towards the welfare of workers seemed calculated to breed discontent. Under the government's protective hand, Russian industrialists were spared the cut-throat competition of English conditions, yet on the whole they resisted the workers' demands for more pay and better conditions, except when under direct pressure of strikes, and then only in boom times. The government was anxious to prevent its hopes for political stability, based on economic prosperity, from foundering on antagonism between the workers and the bosses. Enlightened labour legislation, which the government introduced during the 1880s and 1890s, applied only to factories employing at least twenty people, and in practice was only carried out in very much larger enterprises. The patent intention of the government was to reduce industrial tension where it threatened the greatest repercussions.

Russia's small but highly concentrated working class became in the short time it had existed an object of concern for the regime, which saw in labour discontent a hindrance to rapid modernisation, and hence security for the state. The working class also became an object of concern for the industrial middle class, which saw its own prosperity, social expansion and political potential threatened by the government's supervision of labour relations*. And finally the working class became the object of a small section of the intelligentsia, students and political journalists, who recognised in it the motive force of revolution, as a hopeful alternative to the peasants.

* See references to Zubatov.

I

The First Russian Marxists

A significant section of the Russian intelligentsia found in Marxism the theory upon which they could base their abandonment of the peasantry in favour of the proletariat as the bearer of socialist revolution. But the almost simultaneous arrival in Russia of intensive capitalist industrialisation and Marxism meant that Russia's factory-working class was scarcely born before it became the chosen vehicle of the revolutionary intelligentsia. It had little time to develop its own indigenous institutions, social or political. Russian Marxists held an almost proprietary attitude towards the future development of the Russian working class. But in confronting the economic and political realities in Russia at the turn of the century they saw that their hope of mobilising the proletariat into an organised force under Social Democratic leadership was overshadowed by a paradox.

Marx taught that power would be wrested from autocracy by the capitalist middle class, which would burst its bonds as its economic power outstripped its political rights. In western Europe, Marxists believed, the class struggle was going on between the workers and the bourgeoisie-in-power. In Russia, by contrast, it was the Tsar who was in power and the middle class had still to achieve a great deal of economic headway before it would be strong enough to confront the full might of the Tsarist state. Where, then, should the workers stand? Their true interests could not be realised until the Tsar was overthrown and the struggle against the bourgeoisie culminated in a socialist revolution. This, then, was the paradox. Socialist revolution evolved from class conflict, but in Russia the main enemy was shared also by the workers' class enemy.

By the turn of the century the majority of Social Democrats active inside Russia solved the problem to their own satisfaction by calling upon their fellow socialists to support the middle class in its struggle for a constitution, and at the same time by focussing the workers' attention on economic injustice. Leading Marxist intellectuals had allied themselves with the radical wing of the liberal movement and soon a liberal party would emerge from this alliance. A united front of political opposition to the Tsarist regime was coming into being, and Russian Social Democrats were having to decide where to cast their lot.

If they chose to support the liberal cause they would immediately lose their already threatened monopoly of guiding the workers and their party. If, on the other hand, they advocated political as well as economic warfare against the bourgeoisie they would quickly bring about the isolation of the working class, and the combined enmity of the state and the industrial middle class. The solution, found by the most vocal of the Social Democrats, Plekhanov and his Group 'Emancipation of Labour' in exile, was to aim at organising a Social Democratic mass party of such strength that a combination with the middle-class democratic movement would be possible under working-class leadership. In this combination a strong working class would assist a weak bourgeoisie into power, and at the same time ensure that its own interests were not harmed in the process.

But all this was in the realm of speculation and detachment from the real Russia. The transmission of these ideas to the country for which they were intended was haphazard and in general rather sparse. To commute the Group's abstract formulations into a workers' organisation, a mass party, was beyond the Group's capacities. Dozens of Marxist circles had, it is true, sprung up in Russian towns and cities, and emissaries did travel back and forth between the Group and home, but the Group's most frequent Russian visitors were students from the émigré colonies, young men and women having little or no contact with workers at home, and little idea how to make such contact. Thus it was in western Europe that Russian Marxism, for the most part, developed as a political doctrine.

If a pattern can be discerned in Russian Social Democracy during the last two decades of the nineteenth century, it shows a series of unplanned, 'unscientific' tactical changes by the Marxist revolutionaries, changes which were embellished by new formulations of theory. Theory tended to follow expediency.

In the 1880s, in various Russian towns, Marxist intellectuals began to set up small propaganda circles to educate workers. These circles, later criticised for their inadequacy, were justified as a means of forming a class-conscious and politically mature élite of workers, who would carry the revolutionary torch into the factory, which lay beyond the reach of the intellectual.

However, during the early 1890s workers were staging strikes quite independently of the circles, of Marxist influence or even of the influence of the circle-educated élite. As a result the Social Democrats changed course and a new theory, of mass agitation, was coined. The change was from propaganda to mass agitation, from circles to large, open-air and ostensibly secret assemblies of workers, from intensive political education to widespread pressure by the workers against their employers for everyday needs. This mass agitation was characterised by the Social Democrats as the gradual cultivation in the worker of an awareness of his economic interests, his social importance, and ultimately his political strength. It was also seen as a way of repeating the western pattern, in a very much compressed period of time, and this notion provided the scientific cachet where it may have been felt lacking.

But ceaseless persecution by the police, which kept up a constant decimation of the revolutionary groups and forced survivors to live underground, quickly put paid to the hope that a mass organisation might develop. It became almost impossible to bring Marxist influence to bear on the workers, who succeeded in winning ever more concessions from employers anxious to exploit the economic boom. As a result, Social Democrats began to turn their attention more to the question of their own organisation, rather than that of the workers. It was to be Lenin who, by 1902, made a virtue of this necessity.

Out of the record of disillusion he would salvage the belief that a disciplined party of professional revolutionaries, self-reliant and autonomous in theory and practice, was the only practical and proper course to follow. In the process of creating a Marxist party out of the fragmentary organisation that existed in the nineties, a new and lasting division would be opened up in the radical intelligentsia, and the political organisations of the Russian working class would become the object of two contending sides, Lenin, and his Social Democratic opponents.

The spiritual and theoretical leadership of the Russian Marxist movement arose in western European exile and there it remained until 1917. None enjoyed this position uncontested for as long as Plekhanov and his Group, called Emancipation of Labour, and comprising besides himself the veterans Paul Akselrod, Vera Zasulich and Lev Deich. While all three were intellectuals, the variety of their backgrounds and the range of their personalities formed an exemplary combination for the guidance and inspiration of the overwhelmingly middle-class revolutionary movement, which was seeking to awaken and mobilise the workers.

Georgii Valentinovich Plekhanov (1856–1918) was the son of a small landowner and ex-army officer. Educated in military academies for the chosen career of army officer, at the age of eighteen Plekhanov underwent a quasi-religious crisis prevalent among young men of his background in that period. He awoke to the sufferings of the Russian people and realised that his strong desire to fight their battles would bring him into conflict with his oath of allegiance to his Emperor. He therefore turned from a moderately promising military career to the more socially useful one of engineer.

In the course of his engineering studies in St Petersburg

between 1874 and 1876 he became an active revolutionary Populist. In 1879 when the Populist movement turned to terror as an effective alternative to propaganda, Plekhanov formed his own party, *Chernyi Peredel**, in which education and propaganda were primary aims. For him the weapons of revolution were ideas and it was the function of the intelligentsia to wield them. To transform the outlook of the working masses, which must precede their social and political emancipation, was the first task of the revolutionary movement. Acts of terror perpetrated by the *Narodnaya Volya* (*People's Will*) group, from which Plekhanov's Group had split in 1879, led to intensified police activity, and in January 1880 Plekhanov, together with three other members of his Group, found it necessary to leave Russia for the revolutionaries' haven of Geneva. It was to a vastly changed Russia that Plekhanov, as 'the Father of Russian Marxism', returned thirty-seven years later.

In Geneva in the course of two years Plekhanov abandoned his Populism and became a fully convinced Marxist. His physical detachment from Russia, where Populism had failed in practice, permitted him to devote himself without inhibition to a theoretical assessment of Russian conditions. His natural doubts about the peasants' ability to act rationally and in their own interests found consolation in the Marxist elevation of the factory workers to the vanguard of revolution. In the concept of class struggle he found a substitute for the populist teaching of history as the struggle between the individual and the state, so dramatically applied in terrorism. The future, according to Marx, lay with the development of capitalism, with the organisation of the working class spawned by it, and with the conflict that must arise as a result of the scale of values inherent in capitalism. The logical coherence and scientific certainty of Marxism appealed to Plekhanov, as it would soon appeal to a generation of Russian intellectuals in search of sociological aids and a cause that embodied the scientific mood of the period.[1]

Paul Borisovich (Pinkhas Borukh) Akselrod (1850–1928)

* i.e. redistribution of the black earth.

could hardly have had a background more different from that of Plekhanov. He was one of the several children of an impoverished Jewish innkeeper, living in a small Ukrainian village where hardship for a Jewish family was a compound of poverty, helplessness before the hostile officers of an unsympathetic legal system, and the constant and sometimes violent animosity of the surrounding non-Jewish population. As a bright child he was helped by sympathetic members of a Jewish community to attend a Russian high school. Here he soon picked up the ideas and feelings of social guilt which were current among the Russian intellectuals.

As a youth, Akselrod worked in his own village to bring his Russian light to the talmudic gloom that engulfed the lives of Jewish boys less fortunate than himself. It was on reading Lassalle's works, in which a romantic and idealistic compassion for the poor and downtrodden masses was mingled with a sense of revolutionary messianism, that Akselrod, in 1871, decided to turn his strength towards the emancipation of all the poor and the oppressed of Russia.

His enthusiasm coincided with the great movement 'to the people', of 1872–3, in which he took part with a special sense of pride, rather than indebtedness. From now on he was a full-time revolutionary, but with an abiding belief in propaganda and agitation as the means to awaken and transform the masses. The eventual abandonment by the Populists of work among the masses in favour of individual acts of terrorism against the state, led Akselrod into firm collaboration with Plekhanov at the end of the seventies. His observations, between 1875 and 1879, of the working class in Germany, where he had fled from the Russian police after the failure of the 'to the people' movement, led him to envisage conflict among the nascent industrial forces in Russia, and to his acceptance of Marxism.[2]

Vera Ivanovna Zasulich (1851–1919) brought to the Group its most dramatic link with the heroic tradition of Populism. In 1878 she it was who fired the shot at the military governor of St Petersburg, setting off a series of terrorist acts that culminated in the assassination of Alexander II. In spite (or because) of her genteel background and private education, by the age of sixteen she had become sufficiently rebellious to be actively involved with the legendary terrorist Nechaev*, and by 1869 she had been arrested and sentenced to four years prison and exile. Nothing daunted, she had returned to revolutionary activity, fired her shot at the military governor in 1878, was tried and acquitted by a sympathetic jury, and allowed to escape abroad, where she became a Marxist. Her presence in the Group was as much a mandate from the Russian revolutionary intelligentsia as was Plekhanov's.

The active and, strictly speaking, non-intellectual member of the Group, whose chief value was in linking it with Marxist circles in Russia, was Lev Deich. His untimely arrest in 1884 and the sixteen-year long Siberian exile that followed, deprived the Group of its lifeline to Russia and inaugurated an era of isolation.

The Emancipation of Labour Group was from the outset a source of ideas and inspiration for Marxist circles inside Russia, which sprang up and proliferated under the impact of those ideas. But it remained a remote source, one with which physical contact could be made only sporadically and, for the circles themselves, only vicariously through occasional deputations. Physical distance and the fact that guidance was given in an abstract, literary-ideological way, combined to impart to the Group an almost oracular function.

Plekhanov's role as theoretician of the Russian Marxist movement thus became his sole function, and this in turn produced an exaggerated sense of his own importance which only served to detach him still further from his Russian roots. Plekhanov was wholly dependent on funds raised within the movement, a situation which reinforced his sense of importance. This became a critical factor when, from the middle of the 1890s under the combined impact of intensified police activity and a harsh reactionary attitude in the universities, young Russian students and revolutionaries began to leave Russia in larger numbers to settle in the émigré colonies of the European university towns. Their

* Immortalised as Peter Verkhovensky in Dostoevsky's *The Possessed*.

closer ties with the movement at home, where there was by now some continuity in circles and organisations, their discovery of Plekhanov's authoritarian attitude, and his resentment of any challenge to the position he had held for fifteen years, aggravated relations between the Group and the new generation of Social Democrats, and ultimately made them impossible.

From that time, the middle of the 1890s onwards, the story of the Group is one of continual polemics, short-lived alliances and combinations, violent quarrels, through all of which the embattled trio, Plekhanov—Akselrod—Zasulich, remained somehow intact. The conflict was between generations, for the trio in 1900 had an average age of forty-seven, while the new generation arriving from Russia were men in their early twenties, and were moreover attuned to the changed conditions in Russia which two decades of intensive industrialisation had wrought.

The Marxist circles in Russia failed as a means of reaching the masses through the medium of a few picked and specially educated workers. Instead of a bridge, a barrier was built, and a labour élite split off from the working class. The basic aim of planting even the seeds of political awareness in the working masses was almost as far from realisation as it had been from the Populists of the seventies.

Of one area at least this was not true. In the Pale of Jewish Settlement, Jewish Marxists had some success in organising Jewish workers. There had existed in the Pale, at least since the 1840s, the tradition of mutual aid societies, to offset seasonal fluctuations in employment, and to save for the costs of burial. These funds were based mainly on trades. When Jewish Marxists began to appear in the Pale in the early 1890s, whether despatched there under police orders from Russian universities and high schools,* or home on vacation from their western European studies, the value of the funds as the basis of a real labour move-

* A notable example was Julius Martov, who later became a close collaborator of Lenin's and subsequently Lenin's chief opponent, as leader of the Menshevik faction.

ment dawned on them. After considerable efforts, which were not always welcomed by the workers, the Marxists succeeded in converting the mutual aid societies into strike funds, which became the basic unit of organisation for channelling revolutionary propaganda and agitation. In 1894–5 these tactics were formulated in a pamphlet called *On Agitation* and its ideas were seized on by Marxist organisers in every other centre.

The burden of *On Agitation* was that the working class must engage in political struggle, for without political power it would never improve its lot. But it is futile for the Social Democrats to prod the workers to make political demands for they have no conception of their political interests, all their attention being concentrated on everyday hardships. The workers must be shown that their economic difficulties derive ultimately from their political weakness. For the moment the masses are ready for economic action only, against their employers. Eventually, in their struggle against the bosses, they would be confronted by the police, sent by the state to protect the employers and their property. In that confrontation the workers would see plainly who their real enemy was and political consciousness would dawn on them. The task of Social Democrats is to keep up pressure on the workers to make their economic demands relentlessly, and at the critical moment to turn from economic to political struggle.

In practice this blueprint lost much of its precision. On the workers' side, the concern with working conditions and the sporadic success of the strikes led many of them to regard the intellectuals as both superfluous and dangerous, bringing police interference. Ironically, the police had greater success in organising labour.* Lenin's later complaint, that left to themselves the workers would remain content to consolidate economic gains in trade-union activity, was not groundless. Moreover, workers who had been elevated by the circles to the status of 'intellectual' or 'semi-intellectual' were reluctant to see the system replaced by one in which their new and hard won status would become obsolete. In fact, however, they continued to play a vital part.

* See references to Zubatov.

The functions of maintaining ties between groups were unaltered by the new approach to the workers: organisers remained underground 'professionals', the habits of the circle period, the skills and subterfuges, acquired if anything greater value.

Much more significant for the future development of a Social Democratic movement was the emergence of a new attitude among some intellectuals. Against the background of the widespread political interests and activity among the professional intelligentsia at the turn of the century, many Social Democrats began to consider a wider front of opposition to the regime and constitutional demands. In Germany, where the repeal of Bismarck's anti-socialist laws had recently given reign to freer expression of the demands of the labour movement, socialist thinkers, in particular Eduard Bernstein, were re-examining Marxist theory. Its insistence on class conflict seemed to them to hamper the participation of the working class in the new opportunities being offered. If the dogma of the class struggle prevented collaboration between worker and middle-class democrat in their common aim of a democratic republic, then that particular dogma was an anachronism and should be jettisoned. Marxism was being revised to suit changed conditions in Germany, and in Russia similar 'revisionist' ideas circulated. In Germany the peaceful, gradualist, methods open to the labour movement were nonetheless political, for the strong socialist party was tolerated and there was even a parliamentary group. In Russia, as yet lacking a parliament, the labour movement only had economic tactics open to it and even those were illegal. Russian revisionists therefore advocated economic agitation as the appropriate form of labour's political expression. They were thus dubbed 'Economists' by their enemies, the 'orthodox' Marxists such as Plekhanov and Lenin. The 'Economists' believed they must collaborate with the liberals in their struggle for a constitution. This meant using the legal press as their outlet, and partly as a result of this they became known as Legal Marxists.

For the most part Legal Marxists, or 'Economists', were literary revolutionaries like Peter Struve, Nicolas Berdyaev, Tugan-

Baranovsky and others, whose influence, though considerable, was exercised mainly over other intellectuals, not in the working class.[3] The heated reaction from the 'orthodox' to their defection from the illegal political struggle was, nonetheless, an indication of the importance of the intellectual's role in the movement for political emancipation. The fear among 'orthodox' Marxists that the ideas of 'Economism' would spread among the revolutionary intelligentsia as a whole, provoked a new departure in European Socialism, the Leninist type of Social Democratic party.

From the very outset of the government's policy of rapid industrialisation there began the prolonged and painful history of clashes between the workers and the militia, the strike movement, whose demands for better living and working conditions remained the slogans of Russian labour until 1917 and after. The centre of the Social Democratic movement in Russia was St Petersburg where heavy concentrations of Russia's most urbanised factory workers inhabited the enormous factory barracks of the industrial suburbs. At St Petersburg University there were four times more students than at the next largest, Moscow, and besides the university there were technical institutes, of, for instance, Mining, Technology and Engineering. Full-time revolutionaries were recruited mostly from this large student population. With its Baltic seaport, its proximity by land to Finland and thence to Scandinavia and western Europe, St Petersburg answered many of the needs of a clandestine and hunted organisation, seeking both an outlet and an inlet for its smuggled literature, funds, and agents.

In the course of the 1890s Social Democratic groups had sprung up in virtually every sizeable town in central Russia, as well as in the industrial centres of the Ukraine, the Urals, and in Poland and the western provinces, which today comprise Belorussia, Lithuania, Latvia and Estonia. A network of contacts and a flow, albeit exiguous and intermittent, of help and collaboration between the main cities had developed. By the middle of the nineties groups in St Petersburg, Kiev, Kharkov, Odessa,

Moscow, Vilna and Minsk hoped, with the support of the exile leaders, to build the party. Of these groups the successful Jewish Social Democrats in Vilna were particularly enthusiastic and played an important part in the eventual foundation of the party.

The prominent part and large number of Jews in the Russian revolutionary movement can be explained in a number of ways. One of the most important of these was the disillusionment of the Russian-educated Jewish intellectuals and professionals with the chauvinistic and reactionary policies of Alexander III which followed the promise of emancipation given by his father. The reform movement had been compromised by the assassination of Alexander II, and non-Russian peoples, like 'non-Russian' notions of constitutionalism and democracy, came to serve as a scape-goat for public indignation. Whether or not Alexander III believed the fantastic argument of his advisers that the Jews were behind the discontent of his subjects, he nonetheless opted for the policy that would eventually engender this belief in wide sections of the population. First, violent pogroms were instigated and demonstratively tolerated by the authorities. Special regulations restricted the space available to the Jewish population still further within the already prescribed Pale of Jewish Settlement. To Jewish economic ruin the government added, in 1887, restrictions on education which as much as poverty and civic humiliation fostered in the young an intense hatred of the regime. As an escape from the ardours of the Russian system, hundreds of Jewish students made their way to western Europe, especially Switzerland, and there imbibed the culture and the revolutionary ideals, which in their own country were repressed by the police. In consequence of the government's policy, the educated Jews felt rejected by the country whose culture and language they had assimilated. The identification of their own predicament with the cause of freedom as a whole in Russia was but a single step.*

In 1897, a number of Jewish Social Democratic groups amalgamated in the General Jewish Workers' Union, known as the

---

* Similarly a high number of Polish intellectuals in 'Russian' circles was prevalent until an independent Polish socialist movement developed.

Bund, the first such union of Social Democrats in Russia. The strong desire among Russian Social Democrats to form a party which would deserve representation at the Second International was stimulated by the success of their Jewish comrades, and in March 1898 the All-Russian Social Democratic Workers' Party was founded.* Of the nine delegates, all underground professional revolutionaries, three were from the *Bund* and the others from various Russian centres. None represented the exiled leaders. In general the congress delegates tried to avoid questions of theory, seeing their task rather as the organisational function of bringing the groups together into a party structure. In view of the confused state of Social Democratic theory this was no doubt a wise course.

The Manifesto published in the party's name was written later by Peter Struve, who was not at the congress and who had by then drawn away from Social Democracy towards collaboration with the liberal movement. Struve at that time was thinking of the revolutionary labour movement as the great motive force of the general movement for emancipation in Russia. Although he spoke in the Manifesto of the weakness of the Russian bourgeoisie, it was rather to emphasise the importance of the Social Democratic movement as the dynamo. He was not suggesting that the Russian bourgeoisie was not fit to inherit the political power now residing in the Tsar. Struve referred to the workers' economic interests and the potency of the strike weapon. But the fundamental prerequisite for the gradual improvement of the workers' lot, leading to ultimate emancipation, was political freedom, and it was for that that the proletariat, led by the Social Democratic party, must struggle.

Within a few weeks, the new party's central committee of three, and hundreds of rank and file members, were arrested in a massive swoop, organised by the well-informed secret police. In virtually all but name the party was cancelled out.

* Future references to this title will be in the form of its Russian initials—RSDRP.

2

The Professional Revolutionary

At the turn of the century, the formal existence of the Party
notwithstanding, Russian Social Democracy was in a state of total
disarray. Plekhanov's Group was at odds with the new arrivals
from Russia. The Union of Russian Social Democrats Abroad,
which represented the party officially and published a newspaper
Rabochee Delo (*Workers' Cause*), was, as a result, on the point of
splitting. Mingled with the struggle for control of the movement
that was going on between Plekhanov and the new generation,
was the conflict over tactics and theory that flowed from the new
methods of agitation in Russia. In the eyes of the 'orthodox'
Plekhanov, the questioning of Marx's fundamental tenets threatened to sap the doctrine's revolutionary force. At the rank and
file level in Russia Social Democratic organisations, still styling
themselves committees of the RSDRP, were performing in a
haphazard and 'unscientific' way the habitual tasks of the
revolutionary underground: a little agitation here, a handbill
there. The situation was defined by Lenin as one of *kustarnichestvo*—
completely uncoordinated, primitive, parochial.

If any authoritative control was being exercised over the
organised workers it was by the police. The notion that the government should requisition the revolutionaries' labour policy and
identify with the workers' interests was the brainchild of an ex-
revolutionary, now a senior police official, Sergei Zubatov. He

argued, and he showed in practice, that if the economic demands of the workers were satisfied by the employers, and if the workers were allowed to make their collective claims without fear of attack from the government, their political potential and with it the influence of the Social Democrats, however exaggerated, would evaporate. Strikers arrested by his agents were treated moderately, and Zubatov persuaded them that their real enemies were not the state, but the socialists, who were using them for their own political ends. The workers' needs, he assured them, were genuine and their demands reasonable. Supported by patrons as high up as the Tsar's uncle, Grand Duke Sergei Alexandrovich, Zubatov helped to set up trade unions, which were to act under concealed police·supervision. His agents helped the workers to formulate their demands and then saw to it that employers conceded them.

It was, however, the over-zealous pressure of the police on employers that led eventually to Zubatov's downfall. When in 1903 one of his own unions took the initiative in starting a wave of strikes in southern Russia, Zubatov was blamed and dispensed with, his policy abandoned as dangerous and his unions dispersed. If Zubatovism achieved anything, it was to confirm both the government and the workers in their most firmly held beliefs: for the government, that organised labour was a threat to law and order, and for the workers, that the government was prepared to countenance an alliance with them only so long as it deprived the revolutionary movement of their support. The economics or other interests of the workers were seen to count for nothing. Zubatovism had, in addition, reinforced the belief fairly widespread among workers' organisations, that in general they were themselves best fitted to look after their own interests. The interference of the authorities or of the Marxist intellectuals introduced an entirely alien and undesirable element which could only diminish the prospects of industrial peace and better working conditions.

But if the workers were seeking more congenial channels of self-interest, Social Democrats were equally intent on finding an effective form of organisation which would by-pass existing hazards. Instead of trying to build up the party through the slow, and seemingly doomed process of recruiting members from among the workers; instead of seeking guidance from the exile factions, a new solution was found. Its chief features were that the party organisation should be a small and highly conspiratorial body of full-time professional revolutionaries, recruited predominantly from the student intelligentsia, and exercising control and leadership, sometimes remotely and covertly, sometimes openly, over mass organisations. This two-tier concept arose partly out of the need to safeguard the party organisation against the vicissitudes of Russian police activity, but it also secured for its initiators a degree of autonomy more congenial to their outlook. The most coherent formulation of this idea and its most consistent application were achieved by Lenin.

According to Martov, who was then Lenin's closest collaborator, during the nineties before their exile Lenin had not yet evinced the assertiveness of character and self-righteousness that later became his hallmarks.[1] But Potresov, his other partner at that early period, observed that the twenty-five-year-old Lenin already bore the marks of an old man, was bald, and had the hoarse voice of a middle-aged tradesman. Potresov suggested that this premature ageing, this complete suppression of youthfulness, was grounded in some emotional basis,[2] and subsequent commentators have almost all followed this rational interpretation.

Lenin's personality has exercised as great a fascination over his biographers and historians of the Russian revolutionary movement as over those who observed him at close hand. He was an object of awe long before he succeeded in seizing power in 1917. The basis of this awe and fascination lay in the totality of his commitment to his chosen aims, and in the apparently utter certainty which filled his mind. Even revolutionaries hardened in the martyrdom of the *Narodnaya Volya* were astounded by the degree of his conviction.

Vladimir Ilyich Ulyanov was born on 23 April 1870 in the

provincial town of Simbirsk on the Volga, where his father was schools inspector of the province. Vladimir was the third child in a family of six. The eldest was Anna (born 1864). She became his first official biographer and on her account much of the subsequent literature, whether hagiographic or condemnatory, has been based. After Anna came Alexander (born 1866). Then, after an interval of four years during which a child born in 1868 died shortly after, came Vladimir. He was followed by Olga (1871), Dmitri (1874) and Maria (1878). Not counting Olga, who died aged twenty, the entire family of children became active revolutionaries. Alexander was hanged in 1887 for his part in planning an attempt on the life of the Tsar. The others all devoted their lives to the purposes of the next brother, Vladimir.

The Ulyanovs were not unique as a family of revolutionaries; there was also the Tsederbaum family, which produced Martov and two other brothers who became revolutionaries, as well as the future Lydia Dan; or the Goldman family, in which one brother (Liber) became a *Bundist* leader, another (Leon) ran an illegal press for *Iskra*, while a third (Gorev) was prominent in the first Petersburg Union of Struggle. In addition they had two sisters active in the movement, one of them at one time the fiancée of Dzerzhinsky. Husband-and-wife combinations were of course numerous, almost *de rigueur*, among professional revolutionaries, but whole families were rare.

What was perhaps entirely original about the Ulyanovs was that they all belonged to the same group, indeed constituted a 'tendency' in themselves, and none of them questioned the leadership of the family head, Vladimir. They were all Leninists well before the emergence of a Leninist wing of the party. The circumstances of their brother Alexander's death are universally accepted as a formative influence in Lenin's life, and there is little reason to doubt that all the Ulyanovs were profoundly affected by the shock, coming as it did only one year after the loss of their father. The aura of nobility that before 1881 had surrounded acts of terrorism was much fainter in 1887, and educated society was no longer moved to sympathy by the hanging of a would-be regicide. The Ulyanov family had not escaped the added sense of criminal guilt that would follow an act such as Alexander's. The family's pre-occupation with revolution can be taken as a response more complex than mere vengeance for Alexander's life.

The young Lenin's promising educational prospects were disrupted by this event, for the university authorities at Kazan, where he began his law studies soon after his brother's death, found an early opportunity to expel the bearer of the notorious name. In December 1887, after a two-day imprisonment for participation in a student demonstration, he was thrown on his own resources to complete his studies. Repeated requests by Lenin and his mother to regain admission to the university, or to go abroad to study, met with refusal, but by the end of 1891 he succeeded in gaining, with distinction, his law degree as an external student.

In the meantime, living at the family home in Samara, he had also acquainted himself with the literature of Populism, notably the highly influential didactic novel of Chernyshevsky, *What is to be Done?* which had inspired the movement 'to the people' in the 1870s and was the formative literary experience of the members of 'People's Will', among them Alexander Ulyanov.*

From this source Lenin mainly digested the idea of struggle and the clash of strong wills against the resisting barriers of environment, as the only worthwhile path of human endeavour and as the real content of history.[4] Subtitled 'Tales of the New Men', Chernyshevsky's pamphlet in novel form made it plain that only those who acted in their own untrammelled interest, who were uninhibited egoists and who observed life with the cool detachment of the scientist at his microscope, could expect to contribute to the good of mankind and to the progress of history. That only a few would be capable of undertaking this lonely task was self-evident, but it would be precisely these

* In 1902 Lenin borrowed the title *What is to be Done?* for an exposition of the full body of his organisational views. This work has been recently analysed and newly translated by S.V. and Patricia Utechin.[3]

exceptional people who would point out and lead the haphazard steps of the unwitting masses along the correct path. From Chernyshevsky Lenin learned that, though the 'rotten wall' of Tsarism would be pushed down by the battering ram of the masses, the effort was to be aimed by the planning and intelligence of an élite, the 'new men', the committed revolutionaries.

From old members of the *Narodnaya Volya* exiled in Samara, the young Lenin eagerly imbibed the traditions and techniques of that legendary organisation. Already immersed in the Marxist literature that came to hand, Marx's *Capital* and Plekhanov's polemics against the Populists, Lenin in Samara was going through a process of intellectual transition, common to many ex-Populists and future Marxists of the early nineties. Rejecting the ideas of Populism, they were eager to apply the arts of illegal organisation among the urban proletariat, where the Marxist promise of the future lay.

The exact dates and circumstances of Lenin's conversion from Populism to Marxism are a subject of some argument, but it is plain that the process was complete by the time he moved from Samara to Petersburg in the late summer of 1893. His first Marxist friends in the capital were surprised by his vehement impatience with 'historical process'; like the legendary Zhelyabov, who had been hanged for his part in the assassination of Alexander II, Lenin urged that, as history moves too slowly, it must be given a push. To Lenin the acquiescence of intellectuals in 'inexorable laws' by which the victory of the proletariat over capitalism was guaranteed, spelt doom for a revolutionary party. While his Marxist orthodoxy was already recognised, his zeal as a revolutionary of an earlier tradition, unrelated to the socialism of Marx's western Europe, gave him his stamp.

From Samara Lenin brought with him references which, together with his revolutionary pedigree, introduced him to active Social Democrats in the capital. He became a member of a group run by Stepan Radchenko, together with students of the Technological Institute. For a year his activities were limited to the preoccupations of typical intellectual circles: preparation and discussion of papers and reports on topical questions, on new books of political interest. His contacts with genuine workers, as distinct from a small élite of 'half-intellectual', circle-trained Social Democrats, were still sparse. He found for himself a position as a lawyer, and avoided the risk of regular meetings with workers.

Moreover, his attention was focussed upon making his name as a Marxist theorist among the leading figures in socialist journalism.[5]

Within a year, however, Lenin was devoting himself wholly to his activities as a revolutionary and publicist. He stopped practising as a lawyer and became increasingly involved in the great debate being conducted by the two opposing camps of Marxism and Populism. After only two years he could count himself among the leading exponents of Marxist theory. His interest in the issues confronting Social Democrats took him abroad, in 1895, to visit Plekhanov and Akselrod. His enthusiasm and theoretical assurance heartened the founders of the Russian movement, while their approval and encouragement spurred him to set about establishing the long overdue party in Russia. But it was the return to Petersburg, in the spring of 1895, of Julius Tsederbaum (Martov) which made a greater practical impact on Lenin and his colleagues.

Martov, born in 1873, came from a family of middle-class Jewish intellectuals. His grandfather was a leading figure in the movement for secularising and 'enlightening' Jewish life in Russia. Martov's father was also a journalist, and the family atmosphere is recalled by all the members who left memoirs as cosmopolitan and highly cultivated. Martov had already served a short prison sentence in 1891 when his revolutionary views scarcely went beyond romantic protest. Like Lenin, it was after his university career was cut off that he turned his considerable academic ability to a serious study of Marx and the Marxist writings filtering into Russia from the pens of Plekhanov and Akselrod. Barred from the university but permitted to remain in the capital, by the end of 1892 Martov and his friends constituted a fully-fledged Marxist group, to which they gave the name of the Petersburg Emancipation of Labour Group, in token of their regard for their mentors in exile.

In 1893, after another short spell in prison, Martov was barred for two years from the capital or any other university city. He requested permission to reside in Vilna. By then Vilna was already well known as a centre of interesting developments, with its relatively easy access to Germany, its contacts with the Polish socialists, its higher concentration of initiated workers and, very important, the fact that it was the home of large numbers of Jewish students from Russian and foreign universities, who regularly returned on vacation with ideas and contacts.

The two years spent by Martov in Vilna saw the successful change from propaganda circles run by Jewish Marxist intellectuals to mass agitation of the Jewish workers. Martov was an enthusiastic and influential participant and he returned to Petersburg eager to apply his experience and underground know-how among the Russian workers.

Martov found with dismay that the Social Democrats of the capital were still isolated from the masses. His organisational zeal found an echo in Lenin, newly returned from his conversations with Plekhanov and Akselrod, and anxious to broaden the front well beyond propaganda circles. Martov's influence was decisive in converting the Social Democrats of the capital to the Vilna methods, which at this time other Jewish revolutionaries from Vilna were spreading to other Russian industrial centres.

Martov's loyalties and ties with the Vilna underground remained intact, and his experience had made him one of the most skilful clandestine operators. Lenin and Martov merged their two groups into one, numbering seventeen members, with another five as deputies, ready to take over the organisation in case of arrest.[6] Fourteen were responsible for local-level agitation, the city being divided into regions for this purpose; Radchenko and his wife were responsible for handling the funds, while Lenin, the most accomplished journalist among them all, was responsible for producing all the literature needed for handing out in the factory districts, in secret meetings, and any other possible place. But the group was scarcely able to provoke activity on the factory floor, nor yet capable of exploiting already existing strife.

Thus strikes that took place and to which the group turned its attention were almost completely unaffected by its agitational literature. Its existence was, however, justified by the disproportionate notoriety which its pamphlets and handbills earned it in the eyes of the workers and, still more effectively, in the eyes of the police. In December 1895 ten of the group, including Lenin, were arrested, and in January 1896 another two, including Martov, followed. The work of the group was now the responsibility of the five shadow members. Between the arrest of Lenin and that of Martov the group had been given the name under which it subsequently became famous as the historic origin of the party, the St Petersburg Union of Struggle for the Emancipation of the Working Class. Contrary to legend, Lenin was never active in it while it possessed that title.

Of the latter half of the 1890s it would be no exaggeration to say that the main centres of Russian Marxist and Social Democratic activity were in Western Europe and Siberia. Mass arrests brought about the settlement of whole colonies of revolutionaries in Siberia, who upon release frequently went abroad to augment the already bustling centres of Russian student and revolutionary population in the European university cities.

Apart from some delay in the postal service, there were few obstacles in Siberian exile to maintaining constant contact with one's comrades, either in exile like oneself or still at large, or abroad. Books on any subject could be sent by family and friends, and writings could be sent back to the interior and even published, within the limits of the censorship, under which any writer laboured. Thus in his Siberian exile Lenin was able to concentrate all his attention on literary and academic work. The work he did while in exile in Siberia, where in all he spent three years— February 1897 to February 1900—included his impressive treatise on the history of Russian industrialisation, entitled *The*

Development of Capitalism in Russia. He had collected most of the factual data while serving his preliminary prison sentence of one year in Petersburg before being deported to the east. Also in exile, in the summer of 1898, Lenin married Nadezhda Krupskaya, whom he had met in 1894. Her circle activities had led to her arrest and eventual exile, and she requested to be sent to Shushenskoe, where Lenin was.

The period in Siberia passed agreeably, and Lenin relaxed from his prolific writing by hunting in the woods. Sharing the domestic chores with her mother, who was to live with them until her death in 1915, Krupskaya was content to function as secretary and comrade-in-arms.

Lenin left Shushenskoe on the day his term ended, 29 January 1900, even though his wife had still to serve fifteen months. He lost weight and suffered from sleeplessness in the months prior to his departure, but neither he nor Krupskaya seemed unduly dismayed at so early a rupture in their married life. His nervousness is invariably attributed to his desperate impatience to get to work on the 'burning problems' confronting the movement.

The years of Lenin's exile saw many changes in the Marxist and labour movements, in Russia and abroad. In Germany, Marxist theory was being subjected to a searching reappraisal. The Russian debate over the applicability of Marx's concepts to Russia was exacerbated by this questioning of the dogma.* Particularly important for the revolutionary movement was the doubt being thrown by Bernstein on the progress of the class struggle. The Russian workers were already demonstrating the partial validity of Bernstein's belief, as they showed increasing concern with the purely economic, trade-union, side of their 'social-democratic' activities.

The revolutionaries were not able to do much to reverse the trend. Though the party had been founded in 1898, the arrests which had followed in the ensuing weeks had laid waste to the organisation that had been laboriously built up, and little remained

* See Kindersley, *The First Russian Revisionists* for a definite study of this subject.

of ties, either between cities in Russia or between local committees and leaders abroad. Plekhanov's leadership of the movement had been severely questioned by the new generation of
exiles, and the Group was almost completely estranged from the
party's official representative abroad, the Union of Russian
Social Democrats, to which the younger members tended to adhere.

To Lenin in exile all these developments appeared as symptoms of
a disease which was eating into the vitals of the revolutionary
movement, poisoning the spirit of the great tradition laid down
by *Narodnaya Volya*. He had not decided to devote his life to
revolution in order to help the workers set up trade unions and
mutual-aid societies. Nor would he sit idly by while the armchair
revolutionaries of St Petersburg told the socialist intelligentsia
that the workers had no need of revolutionary organisations of
their own, but must instead be helped to form themselves into
unions which would openly support the liberals in their struggle
for reforms against the Tsarist autocracy. This, to him, was
tantamount to handing over one's ammunition to the enemy,
for in a liberal victory he saw the greatest danger to socialist
revolution. His equal distrust of the working class made it
impossible for him to see any other outcome to a liberal success
than the seduction of the workers by bourgeois freedom, parliamentary humbug and deception, social swindle through economic
bribery.

The circulation in 1899 of a document, known as *Credo*, by
Elena Kuskova, which for Lenin typified these ideas, prompted
him to plan for an all-out offensive to wipe out the heretics and
restore the movement to a healthy revolutionary path. The chief
characteristics of this path were: complete cohesion of all Social
Democratic elements in hostile distinction to all liberal reform
efforts; ruthless exclusion from the Social Democratic press of
heretical, that is critical, points of view; and for the workers'
consumption, 'politics before economics' that is, 'the overthrow
of Tsarism' as a slogan of greater priority than the call for an
eight-hour day and similar ephemera.

Instead of vulnerable circles of dedicated intellectuals, Lenin planned an underground newspaper, written and backed by the great names of the unadulterated tradition, which would spread the message. Lenin's newspaper was to act as a banner, on which would be inscribed 'Orthodoxy'. Its purpose would be to rally dedicated revolutionaries who were loyal, not to the cause of reform and constitution, but to that of total destruction of the existing order in Russia. The paper was to be called *Iskra* (*The Spark*). It would be carried into and around Russia by a small but growing group of tested professional revolutionaries, whom Lenin and Martov mostly recruited to their cause in Siberian exile, or in their towns of banishment in the provinces. A common characteristic of these *Iskra* 'agents' was their lack of local ties. They were unencumbered, uprooted, and prepared for a life of unending mobility. All were by definition experienced hands at illegal survival, and already had their own contacts. The force of Lenin's personality and the complete conviction he expressed acted as a binding influence on the men he recruited for his underground network.

Leaving Martov in Russia to set up local facilities and rally supporters, Lenin went to Switzerland to enlist Plekhanov's backing for his plan. Lenin wanted Plekhanov's Group to publish a theoretical journal to pronounce the orthodox word to the movement and to demonstrate the ideological purity of the Russian party to the socialist parties of the west; Lenin and his friends would produce *Iskra*, the newspaper which would be in intimate contact with the local committees of the party in Russia, would act as a *de facto* central committee, on which the locals would gradually become ideologically and materially dependent. Like Plekhanov's journal, called *Zarya* (*Dawn*), *Iskra* would be published in the safety of western Europe. The constant flow of agents to and from the groups in Russia was, thus, an essential condition for the success of this venture. It was only through the personal visit of the agent that the local committee could be sure of receiving *Iskra* and, of equal importance, feel that it was part of a widespread, viable organisation. This system, which could only function on trust, naturally tended to exaggerate the power both of the agents and of the remote leaders.

Lenin's pretension to leadership of the party in Russia was matched by his sense of equality with the 'Father of Russian Marxism', Plekhanov. Hope of collaboration failed when Lenin was confronted by a domineering Plekhanov, whose reluctance to become one of a team was matched by Lenin's determination to keep the initiative. Eventually it was agreed to set up a common editorial board consisting of Plekhanov, Akselrod and Zasulich for the Group's journal *Zarya*, and Lenin, Martov and Potresov for *Iskra*. Lenin and his friends, however, would set up *Iskra* in Munich, at a safe distance from Plekhanov. Their first issue appeared in December 1900.

3

The Socialists Organise

In the years 1901 to 1903 *Iskra*'s organisation ramified and strengthened itself in the local committees. On the ideological level its appeal for the agitation of the masses, as distinct from economic protest, certainly drew the most militant revolutionaries, many of them old Populists. But more than doctrine the regularity of its appearance and increasing certainty of delivery, as well as the technical aid its agents could often furnish to committees in the way of passports and literature, gradually forged bonds between the *Iskra* network and the local organisations.

But since Lenin and his colleagues were waging war against impurity in the party, *Iskra* had to weed out, or at least mark, likely dissidents with one hand, while recruiting new members with the other. When necessary, the material benefit brought by *Iskra* was used as a lever to split an 'infected' committee, isolate the dissidents, commandeer what local facilities might exist, for instance a press, and then publish a statement pledging the committee to *Iskra* and to *Iskra*'s 'line'. This technique was the keystone of Lenin's campaign for preparing the party for its Second Congress. Mandates to the congress were confirmed by a special Organisational Committee, set up in Russia in 1902 by an emissary from Lenin, with the main object of acting as an acid test, a filter through which committees could gain access to the congress only if they had satisfied the committee's requirements. These were: renunciation of *Workers' Cause*, published by the Union of Russian Social Democrats Abroad, as the official organ of the party; recognition of *Iskra* in its stead; and acceptance of *Iskra*'s plan for a new, centralised structure of the party.

Faced with recalcitrance, Lenin's agents were instructed to fabricate their own local committee, or faction, and grant it the mandate which rightly belonged to the indigenous organisation. Ruthlessness was exercised by *Iskra*'s agents, sometimes reluctantly, to achieve Lenin's target, but almost always these tactics were used only with small provincial committees; there a change could be effected rapidly, before it could be taken up as an issue by *Iskra*'s more powerful enemies. Elsewhere, as in the case of the *Bund* and the large and powerful *Southern Worker* organisation based on industrial centres in the Ukraine, Lenin strained to preserve a façade of legality for his actions. His letters to his agents bristle with warnings to be careful, and to pay strict respect to formalities which were particularly important at a time when suspicions were easily aroused and trust was a valuable asset.

It was during these two intensive years of campaigning, mainly by correspondence, of which a prodigious amount has been published,[1] that Lenin revealed his genius for underground organisation. He also revealed his disregard for human values, treasuring only one dimension of human activity: service. From his agents, and, as it transpired, from his colleagues too, he expected the same selfless and unquestioning service which, he imagined, he himself devoted to the cause of revolution. In his letters to his secret agents he urged them to dissemble, to lie and deceive, threaten and appease, in order to obtain declared support for *Iskra*. Genuine ideological conversions were less valuable than the ritual performed for the sake of admission to the coming congress. To Lenin the value of a conversion lay in the published signed statement of it, to be used as an advertisement to others yet unconvinced. The great *Iskra* campaign was little more than a method of vote-catching, except that the process was to continue in the congress, when *Iskra* would be duly elected by its own appointees.

What was this congress meant to achieve? First and foremost it was to provide a formal and 'legitimate' investiture of the *Iskra* organisation as the central nervous system of the entire party. This would be done by electing a central committee and an editorial board from candidates sponsored by the *de facto* leadership and supported by the majority of the delegates, themselves already pledged to that leadership. Since *Iskra* had never been accorded any official status in the party, and the connection of most of the committees attending the forthcoming congress with the original party of 1898 was purely imaginary, establishing the title of the congress as the 'second' was a matter of psychological importance.

To perhaps a majority of the delegates the congress was expected to provide the full definition of their purpose, to give form and structure to their work and to the party in whose name they risked their liberty. After five years of nominal existence the Party had yet no programme, no statutes for its own organisation and no rules governing the relations of the centre with the local committees. Although the full congress would confront these tasks, the *Iskra* organisation had been proclaiming itself the sole arbiter of such matters for the past two years.

The congress opened in Brussels in July 1903, and after one week of police harassment, moved to London. Of the fifty-seven delegates to this proletarian party's congress, no more than three or four were themselves workers. Moreover, they had been elected in secret session by their committees, without the knowledge or participation of the rank and file.[2] Lenin had reconciled, to his own satisfaction, the need for legitimacy with a guaranteed monopoly for *Iskra* by allowing his known enemies minimal representation. Thus the *Bund*, with its membership of 30,000 and its long history of effective organisation, was given a mere five votes; and the dissident *Workers' Cause*, the official representative of the party in exile, was given three votes, of which only one belonged to its supporting workers' faction from

Petersburg. When the congress met, Lenin felt confident of the support of at least eighty per cent of the delegates.

Thus the levels of concealment and imposture at this meeting were multiple. They ranged from the very name of the congress and that of the party it claimed to represent, down to the fiction of *Iskra*'s homogeneity, for it would quickly emerge that among the Iskraists Lenin had forged his own personal following which would remain loyal to him when the majority had come out against him.

The feverish attention which Lenin had paid to the preparation of delegates in the months before was precisely aimed at ensuring a smooth course for his plans. And to prevent 'accidents' during the congress his vigilance never flagged. He was never absent, and was one of the three most vociferous speakers, matched only by Martov, and Liber, the *Bund*'s spokesman. The proceedings continued for over three weeks—(the longest congress in the party's history)—during a sweltering summer, first in Brussels and then in London. Throughout Lenin made notes and calculations, analysed trends and phrased resolutions, accompanying his jottings with scribbled expletives of irony and sarcasm, impatience and triumph. No other delegate was so diligent and nobody else took the trouble that he did to retrace and explain every step made by the congress after it was all over.

The task of eliminating the opposition presented few problems. The majority had been well briefed. Indoctrination and discipline of his supporters over the question of the *Bund* had figured first on Lenin's private agenda long before the congress met. At the congress itself much effort was expended by *Iskra*'s managers to maintain resistance to *Bundist* overtures among the non-*Bundist* Jewish delegates, who together with the *Bundists* numbered exactly half the votes.[3] And even though the *Bund* succeeded in opening up some chinks in *Iskra*'s armour on the issues of nationality and regional organisations, when it came to the vote on the *Bund*'s continued representation of the Jewish workers in the party, not a single vote was cast in its favour. At the twenty-seventh session the *Bund*'s leaders announced its exit from the congress and from the party it had helped to found. But before this happened the *Bund*'s five votes had been an important factor in the decomposition of Lenin's majority.

The first sign of trouble came at the very outset, not in open session, but in the first of a series of private meetings of the sixteen innermost Iskraists. There Martov expressed the view that in its present position of power *Iskra* could afford to lend a show of representativeness to the congress by sharing the presidium with the opposition. Lenin would not hear of it and insisted that *Iskra* retain the whiphand of authority throughout. Lenin had his way and nothing more was said. But Martov was beginning to develop an undercurrent of suspicion and repulsion towards his former friend. His sense of loyalty was affronted by Lenin's abusive dismissal of respected comrades as candidates for office, and no less by Lenin's steamrolling of objections by his closest supporters. In short, while Lenin was just getting into his stride Martov was beginning to have doubts and to draw back.

The delegates first became aware that something was amiss when it was announced that two versions were being submitted for approval of the statute determining membership of the party, one from Martov and the other from Lenin. This took place during the twenty-second session of the congress, after a great number of important issues had been settled, including the programme. The difference between the two versions seemed marginal. Lenin's draft declared a party member to be one who recognised the programme and supported the party by taking part in one of the party's organisations. Martov defined a member as one who accepted the party programme, gave material support to the party and regular personal support under the guidance of one of its organisations. However vague the difference may now seem to be, the delegates were quick to catalyse the nuances and they produced the simple dichotomy: Lenin wants a narrow party, while Martov wants a broad one.

The main protagonists began their debate with relative calm, indeed almost in the 'wrong corners'. Martov spoke of the party as the conscious expression of an unconscious process, and all his demands for the spread of mass organisations and a broad Social Democratic workers' party, were coupled with the recognition that the core and conscious nucleus of such party institutions was the conspiratorial centre. He was echoing Lenin's *What is to be Done?* when he said: 'Let there be a host of organisations . . . *They cannot enter the party organisation*, but the party cannot do without them.'[4] Here the distinction of the *inner party* was clear.

Lenin opened by trying to calm the atmosphere: 'There's no need to imagine that party organisations must consist only of professional revolutionaries. We need the most varied kinds of organisations . . . from extremely narrow, clandestine ones down to extremely broad, free and open ones. The essential qualification of a party organisation is its recognition by the Central Committee.' All Lenin seemed here to be saying was that the party, represented by its Central Committee, has the right to know and acknowledge those calling themselves its members.

However, once the debate got going and the delegates rose to air their views, a clear division of forces lined up behind Lenin and Martov in opposing camps, and in the mounting pressure of fatigue and personal antagonism the poles of opinion moved further apart.

The root of Martov's mistake, claimed Lenin, was in perpetuating the very evil they had laboured to uproot: they must in future be able to sort out the chatterers from the doers, among both intellectuals and workers. Lenin reminded the congress of the mutual responsibility of the party and its members, and declared that such responsibilities could not be dispensed to all and sundry. Control must be kept exclusively in the hands of the Central Committee.

In this last maxim was enclosed the nub of Lenin's approach: there could be no party activity whatever that was not under the direct control of the centre, the conspiratorial nucleus, of which he was the master. When at last the vote revealed that Martov had a majority, Lenin began a feverish campaign of personal lobbying among the Iskraists. His zeal and conviction which had once been of value as a binding element, now hardened the rift between factions. Lenin's chief weapon was his opponent's inconsistency. Martov had all along supported the ideas embodied in Lenin's position and had himself practised and defended the principle of the professional party. Now with his more liberal statute for membership he was open to the accusation of opportunism.

At the height of the conflict behind the scenes, the congress was faced with having to vote for or against granting the *Bund* the right of sole representation of Jewish workers in the party. The *Bund*'s five votes were the difference between the two *Iskra* factions. But Martov remained faithful to his stated principles on that issue and so did Lenin, who was indeed counting on the outcome. The *Bund* was roundly defeated and left the congress, and the party. It also left Martov minus five votes, to be decreased still further by three when he helped Lenin push out the delegates from the *Workers' Cause*. Martov's high-mindedness, or lack of political acumen, noted by Lenin, was a clear indication of the difference between them. For Martov the congress was an occasion to express and formulate the party's programme, policy, statutes, to proclaim its principles. For Lenin it was the occasion for procuring an oath of allegiance from the party's leading members to its centre.

With the departure of the old opposition the congress became a battleground between the allies. The debates now bristled with mutual recrimination. Lenin was accused of 'Jacobinism', 'Bonapartism' and of wanting to set up a staff of 'generals without an army'. The Martov minority were castigated for 'anarchy', 'irresponsibility' and 'opportunism'. Above all Lenin was now determined to protect the vital centres, the editorial board and the central committee, from the 'democratism' which, in Lenin's opinion, Martov's hysteria threatened to bring. First he pushed through a change making the editorial board supreme in the party, and then proposed the election of a new board consisting of himself, Plekhanov and Martov, thus casting aside the three least productive members of the original board, Potresov,

Zasulich and Akselrod. So much emotional clamour greeted this that the board left the chamber in order to liberate discussion. The delegates, however, spent their time insisting to each other that they had nothing embarrassing to say and their words eddied in meaningless circles. When they voted on whether to reaffirm the old board, however, an undisclosed majority came out negative. The old board returned to the chamber and Martov stated on his own behalf and that of his fellow-ex-editors, Akselrod, Potresov and Zasulich, that they would accept no part in any new board elected on the proposed basis of three members. The *Iskra* board thus consisted of Plekhanov and Lenin.

Martov was determined to stop, if he could, Lenin's march to power. 'Everybody knows', he revealed, 'that the issue here is not "efficiency" [of the abandoned editors], but that it is the struggle for influence over the Central Committee. Because the majority of the board did not want the Central Committee turned into a weapon of the editorial board, it was necessary (for Lenin) to reduce its size.'[5] This point is reinforced by one anti-Leninist who stated baldly that he was astonished to hear mention of 'principles' at this late stage of the proceedings. 'Surely everyone knows that the debates of the last few days have not pivoted on questions of the principles involved, but entirely upon how to ensure or obstruct access to the central institutions of this or that person.' Even Martov smiled when this frank speaker added that 'principles were long lost sight of at this congress and so we can call a spade a spade'.[6]

Lenin succeeded in getting a central committee composed of three of his own supporters. His faction was now master of the congress. From this tiny majority which ruled for only a few last sessions, Lenin took the name of his faction—Bolsheviks (Majorityites)—and bequeathed to Martov the name more fitted in reality to Lenin's own group—Mensheviks (Minorityites). Bertram Wolfe made a penetrating point when he wrote that Lenin would never relinquish the psychological advantage of that name.[7] 'A name, he knew, was a program, a distilled essence, more powerful in its impact upon the untutored mind than any propaganda slogan. . . . If he had remained in the minority, he would have chosen some other banner name—like "True Iskrists" or "Orthodox Marxists". . . . But it is characteristic of his opponents that they permanently accepted the designation of Mensheviki (Minorityites) for their group.'

The congress petered out from exhaustion and animosity. Important points of principle were passed almost with a nod of the head, and a pretence at a business-like winding-up could scarcely hide the atmosphere of wrung-out spirits, jaded palates and the sense of futility that followed upon so much emotional violence. Lenin's victories all turned out to have been no more than the rituals he himself arranged. Allegiances pledged by the show of a hand in a heated debate were soon withdrawn once their donors had had time to reflect and once fresh contact had been made with the world outside the congress. Very soon after the congress Lenin found himself outside the apparatus he had himself created.

While the Social Democrats engaged in endless debate, a separate development was taking place in Russian socialism, that was at once more dramatic and more spontaneous. The turn of the century was marked by pronounced unrest and agitation in three sectors of society: the students, the workers and the peasants. Student demonstrations, workers' strikes and peasant outbreaks, while distinct and unrelated, had the combined effect of producing an atmosphere of expectancy. This coincided with the return from Siberian exile of a number of *Narodnaya Volya* (*People's Will*) veterans, who discerned the signs of a national awakening and proceeded to reorganise themselves for direct action towards general armed uprising and socialist revolution.

By 1902 the Socialist Revolutionary Party had been formed in Geneva, and within a year was reaching a wide area in Russia with its propaganda literature and its regular newspaper, *Revolyutsionnaya Rossiya* (*Revolutionary Russia*), though its programme and party statutes were not formulated until 1906. While the Socialist Revolutionaries experienced almost as much difficulty over doctrine as did the Social Democrats, now torn into factions, they at least were propelled by a much stronger will *to act* in a revolutionary manner and worry about theory when something had been achieved. They were, indeed, far less encumbered with theorists than the Social Democratic party, and most of the Socialist Revolutionary theory and policy was the product of Victor Chernov alone.

Their dedication to the principle of terror is often depicted as their least important feature, and there is no doubt that their propaganda among the peasants was of inestimable importance. But it is worth noting that dramatic, or melodramatic, acts of terror, perpetrated against prominent state officials, had the result, otherwise almost unknown in Russia, of invariably provoking some measurable reaction from the government. The terrorists themselves could derive satisfaction from having made a direct impact on the state. But more important, society at large could pause to wait and see how the regime would take this direct assault. And often, if not invariably, the government would indicate its future intentions towards society as a whole by the manner in which it recovered from individual acts of terror. Thus though no captured terrorist could expect clemency, much could be gauged from the nature of the victim's successor.

This justification for the use of terror echoed the beliefs of the *Narodnaya Volya*, who had held that terror was the symbol of the masses' collective anger. In the 1870s the terrorists had been isolated from society and society itself had been in harmony with the liberal reforms of the government. Now, however, on the eve of 1905, society was in a condition to be excited, even if also appalled, by terrorism, and the new Socialist Revolutionary interpretation of terror was that it was no longer a substitute for mass anger, but was to be its stimulant.

A special 'combat organisation' was set up in 1901 to act autonomously, with its own funds and with supreme priority in the party. Its task was to pick out and assassinate leading government figures. Local units were also set up, and were even more prolific in their assassinations than the central organisation, although the latter group held an undoubted lead for 'quality', numbering among its victims: one minister of education, two ministers of the interior, including, in 1904, Plehve; a powerful uncle of the Tsar, and a number of provincial governors.

The central unit was master-minded by three outstanding terrorists, Evno Azef, Boris Savinkov and Grigory Gershuni. Their success, however, turned out to owe much to the fact that, since the 1890s, Azef had been playing a double role, as police agent as well as revolutionary. He was so diligent in both roles that it remains an open question, which cause he put first. The fact that he cared greatly about his luxurious standard of living, suggests that money was the most immediate motive for his dual treachery. From 1903 until 1908, when he was finally unmasked, Azef controlled the central unit, and was its link with the party Central Committee, on which he also sat. His exposure as an *agent provocateur* shook the Socialist Revolutionary party to its foundations and led directly to its accepting the more peaceful task of propaganda in the villages as its main occupation.

Azef himself, in the company of his mistress (an ex-cabaret singer and demi-mondaine), hid from the fury of his comrades in various Mediterranean luxury hotels, finally settling in Berlin, where he proceeded to augment his considerable Russian capital, as a stockbroker. The war reduced his capital to ruins and instead he and his companion opened a fashionable corset shop. In 1915 he was put in prison, not as he thought for his earlier connection with the Russian police, but for being a 'dangerous revolutionary'. Released a sick man in December 1917, upon the German-Russian armistice, he worked for a short time in the German Foreign Ministry, a position still unexplained, and in April 1918 died unmourned, but not forgotten as the most spectacular example of Russian *agents provocateurs* known to that cynical trade.[8]

Apart from their legitimate claim to be the heirs of *Narodnaya Volya*, the Socialist Revolutionaries became powerful poachers on Social Democratic territory thanks also to the one clear objective which stood out among the rather diffuse body of Socialist Revolutionary doctrine: the overthrow of the Tsarist autocracy by means of mass armed uprising. Their populism, which repudiated the restrictions of class struggle, embraced a much wider revolutionary front than Marxism which surrounded the proletarian vanguard of revolution with class enemies on all sides. The Socialist Revolutionaries, on the contrary, envisaged an offensive alliance of all opposition elements, including even the liberal intelligentsia. Their attitude won them support among the zemstvo specialist employees.

Central to the Socialist Revolutionary psychology was the popular belief that Russia's destiny was to be unique, that it was meaningless to project her future along the course already taken by Europe. Immutable laws of history concerned the Socialist Revolutionary theorist only to the extent that he could turn them on his Marxist critics. The Socialist Revolutionaries recognised that capitalism in Russia had made enormous strides in the latter years of the nineteenth century, but they regarded this as a catastrophe for Russia's socialist prospects. Echoing the populist socialists of the mid-nineteenth century, the Socialist Revolutionaries claimed that the promise of Russia's socialist future lay in the peasant and in his collectivist outlook, embodied in the commune.

Their propaganda and agitation in the villages was aimed at the earliest possible mobilisation of the peasants against further encroachments by capitalism into the countryside. The destructive influence of capitalism on the village, they believed, took various forms: it turned free craftsmen and artisans into journeymen, labouring for remote entrepreneurs from the city; the expanding wealth of the large estates, which prospered in Witte's export drive, was turning the peasantry increasingly into a pool of wage labour, and thereby hastening the decline of the commune.[9]

Against this sombre background the Socialist Revolutionaries further discerned the growing disparity between rich and poor peasants, a fact which was most alarming, since the idea of class struggle inside the village struck at the very root of Socialist Revolutionary populist faith. The main burden of their argument with the Marxists on this issue was that, although capitalism had made inroads, as long as it and the mentality of private ownership were still primitive in Russia it was the duty of socialists to hasten revolution. The drive among the peasants for individual ownership and cultivation of the land was interpreted by the Socialist Revolutionaries as a deviation wrought by the evils of capitalist agriculture, which must be halted by revolution and the 'socialisation' of all land. This process of turning over the land to the peasant, who would then own and cultivate it *collectively*, was intended to restore the allegedly traditional relationship of the Russian peasant to the land he tilled. The agrarian programme conceived by the Socialist Revolutionaries combined, paradoxically, their most utopian and their most appealing aims; the peasants could not resist the promise of *land* and they overlooked the nebulous idea of 'socialisation'; yet this idea was the heart of Socialist Revolutionary doctrine.

The Marxists, not imagining that they would one day adopt this programme as their chief weapon to power, repudiated innate peasant collectivism, and postulated, on the contrary, a deep-seated 'petty-bourgeois' trait in the peasant mentality, which would, first, express itself in personal land-grabbing, and secondly, in opposition to socialist government.

'Socialisation' also applied to industry, in the Socialist Revolutionary blueprint. Here they projected a system of workers' cooperatives, the prototype of which was the small artisan workshop, or *artel*, where, in Socialist Revolutionary eyes, the intimacy of workman and product was a barrier against the further intrusion of capitalist alienation into the working class. This notion was no less utopian, coming as it did after the massive expansion of industry in Russia during the 1890s, than it seems today. More strikingly than the Socialist Revolutionary agrarian policy it demonstrates that they were less concerned to apply their thoughts seriously to the post-revolutionary future of Russia, than to the business of making a revolution, for whatever reason.

At first the Social Democrats, represented by Plekhanov, welcomed the appearance of the new party as blood-brothers, of

Narodnaya Volya pedigree. But as soon as it dawned upon them that the Socialist Revolutionaries had no intention of submitting to Social Democratic leadership, but meant to strike out on their own account, abuse was hurled and whole seams of theoretical inconsistency and nonsense were excavated by the Social Democrats out of Socialist Revolutionary doctrine. The entire programme and activity of the Socialist Revolutionary party was defined by Lenin as '*nothing less than an attempt by the petty-bourgeois intelligentsia to filch our labour movement and, as a result, the whole socialist and revolutionary movement in Russia*'.[10] He made it plain that this would lead quickly to the demise of the movement, and that only those whose work had created it, in other words the Social Democrats, should lead it. The Socialist Revolutionaries clearly constituted a threat to the Social Democrats, but the fact was that neither of these socialist parties held sway over peasant, worker, or intellectual, to the extent that the liberal movement did.

The mouthpiece of liberalism was the journal *Osvobozhdenie* (*Liberation*), first issued in June 1902 by Peter Struve, in collaboration with Paul Milyukov. Published in Stuttgart, it was smuggled illegally into Russia where its platform of radical liberal views quickly gained a wide audience, particularly among the zemstvo employees. On the basis of his success, in June 1903 Struve formed the Union of Liberation, a loose federation of like-minded organisations advocating, among other things, constitutional monarchy, civil rights, and universal suffrage.

When strikes and unrest in the spring of 1903 forced the promise of concessions from the government, *Liberation* gained still greater popularity. Its broad, classless point of view was acceptable to a growing public which was seeking change without upheaval. After spring 1903 the zemstvos began pressing the government to allow them a hand in preparing new legislation. Thus *Liberation* and the zemstvo movement were, in the years 1903–4, speaking with a common voice.[11] There was little either the Social Democrats or the Socialist Revolutionaries could do to wrest the initiative from the successful liberals.

4

State and Society in 1905

The open provocation of Japan practised by the Russian government stands out as perhaps the prime example of gross irresponsibility committed under the last Tsar. Unrest had been mounting among the peasants, the factory-workers and students, and, together with the campaign in the liberal press calling for radical reforms to meet the situation, all contributed to a background of extreme instability. Yet in the midst of so much political and social clamour the government saw fit to entertain a policy of aggressive military and economic expansion in the Far East that virtually ensured a military response from Japan, whose economic interests were most sharply threatened. Where Witte had advocated gradual economic infiltration into the area, Nicolas II succumbed to the advice of less patient men, courtiers with business connections and interests in the Far East, and of his cousin, Kaiser Wilhelm II, who encouraged Nicolas to claim Russia's inheritance in the east, while he, Wilhelm, would safeguard his western frontiers. These blandishments accorded with Nicolas's own dream of himself as heir to the Muscovite tradition of eastward expansion, and Christian missionary to Asia. Witte's persistent opposition led to his dismissal in August 1903. Pressure built up with each new Russian provocation, and finally, at the end of January 1904, the Japanese made a surprise attack on the Russian warships lying at Port Arthur.

So plainly provocative had Russian policy been and so flimsy its justification as imperial benefit that there was widespread belief that the Tsar, encouraged by his Minister of the Interior, Plehve, was making war solely to divert opposition pressure onto something external. Though this was not in fact the case, the government did its best to turn opposition opinion into patriotic feeling. If we discount the enormous peasant population, to which war meant nothing but military service, and the revolutionary movement, there was indeed something of a change of heart, notably among the liberals, which harmonised with a wave of patriotic emotion in society.

The promise of a quick and crushing victory over 'tiny' Japan prompted the liberals to tone down their demands. The regime would be enormously strengthened by the anticipated victory, so that any demand for greater freedom after the war had better be paid for in advance, when the value of help and support was inflated. Thus at first the liberals gained permission to organise the care of the wounded and aid the families of the fallen. Plehve, who discerned the ulterior motive, opposed concessions of this nature and did his best to disrupt such voluntary work.

The calculations of all sides were upset by the news from the front, where Russian forces were undergoing one humiliating setback after the other. Believing that Japan would not dare to attack, the war party at the court had promoted its case before the main supply line, the Trans-Siberian railway, was complete. Nor was the army's position helped by the deep cleavage of opinion and authority at the highest level of command, where political power was vested in the pro-war Viceroy Alexeev, while military command was in the hands of the more circumspect Kuropatkin. By April 1904 Japan had succeeded in splitting the main Russian land forces, isolating the garrison of Port Arthur, and simultaneously immobilising the Port Arthur fleet by mine-fields and destroyer patrols. The Port Arthur naval force was also thus kept apart from that at Vladivostok, 1,000 miles up the coast. As the Japanese drew their land forces closer to a siege of the garrison port, the need to make a naval breakthrough became more desperate. In August an attempt was made, but the entire squadron was immediately put out of action. Port Arthur came under siege and finally surrendered in December 1904. The campaign of the main land force in Manchuria, under Kuropatkin, was no more glorious. Outnumbering the Japanese by 220,000 to 160,000, but dependent upon an inadequate supply line, Kuropatkin's forces could do nothing against the enemy.

Throughout 1904, as defeat followed defeat, public opinion, far from the fronts, was undergoing a process of polarisation. Nationalist feelings were reawakened by the humiliation of defeat; moderates were torn by the sense of duty to throne and father-land and the growing belief that the war was a failure because of corruption, at which the government was conniving; the liberals now saw that the post-war government was not likely to be as popular and powerful as they had once anticipated and they began to calculate the benefit of defeat. The government itself, and consequently the regime as a whole, became the target once again of national dissatisfaction with the war, voiced by the political opposition. By the summer of 1904 Russian public opinion was ready to agree with the thought Lenin had expressed at the outbreak of the war, in his *Address to the Russian proletariat*: 'This will be a struggle between a despotic backward [Russian] govern-ment and a nation [Japan] that is politically free and rapidly progressing culturally.'[1] Japan's victories over the Russian forces seemed to confirm Lenin's (largely unheard) thesis.

The socialist attitude to the war, whether Bolshevik, Men-shevik or Socialist Revolutionary, was essentially that it was a crime perpetrated by the Tsarist government against the Russian people, that it must be frustrated by every means, and that as it continued it would expose the rot of the system, which would be unable to sustain the enormous effort involved. But the socialists themselves were unable to do much towards bringing the war to an early close.

Lenin, after recovering from the nervous exhaustion that resulted from the major setback of the split, devoted his greatest efforts during 1904 and the early part of 1905 to organising his faction for the next 'party' congress, which even more than the Second, was intended to be Lenin's own. Like Lenin, the Mensheviks paid only scant attention to the war in practical terms, though with their superior literary resources and facilities for getting people and literature into Russia, they were in a better position to publicise the party point of view.

The Bolsheviks did, however, undertake a measure of active subversion of the war effort. They disseminated Marxist revolutionary propaganda among Russian prisoners-of-war in the Far East. The vehicle of this propaganda was a Bolshevik journal, *Rassvet (Dawn)*, originally founded by one of the most learned of Bolsheviks, Vladimir Bonch-Bruevich, to attract support among dissident religious groups.*

The Bolsheviks also had some connection with an attempt at an armed uprising. The Japanese were financing the ambitious plans of the Finnish nationalist revolutionary, Konni Zilliacus, who was trying to unite the entire Russian opposition into one offensive alliance against the regime. His efforts resulted in a conference, held in Paris in September 1904, boycotted by the Social Democrats, at which the leaders of the Union of Liberation swore an alliance with the Socialist Revolutionaries (among them Azef), and with the main nationalist revolutionary parties. But while it seemed like serious business to them and was destined to have far-reaching consequences, things were moving too slowly for Zilliacus and he began instead to organise a massive shipment of arms into Russia.

His closest collaborators in this venture were, naturally, the Socialist Revolutionaries, and to a considerable degree also the Bolsheviks. Arms, mostly obsolete, were bought in Switzerland and shipped through the Baltic in the subsequently notorious and slightly hilarious voyage of the *John Grafton*. The ship and most

* Vadim Medish, 'Lenin and Japanese Money', in *Russian Review*, 24, 1965, pp. 169–70, asserts that this operation was financed by the Japanese Government. This view is contested by Michael Futrell in an article in *St Antony's Papers, No. 20: Far Eastern Affairs: Four*, 1967, based on Japanese. as well as the Russian, materials.

of its cargo ended up on the bottom of the Baltic, though some weapons eventually found their destination.[2] But against the background of mounting social protest and the tension produced by traditional Socialist Revolutionary tactics of individual terrorism, this type of enterprise, of which there were others no more successful, was small beer.

The biggest impulse given to events in 1904 came not from arms or explosives smuggled in by the Socialist Revolutionaries, but from their assassination of Plehve, in July. The act was carried out under the direct planning and supervision of Azef himself. One of a series of spectacular assassinations, it was generally regarded as the most effective blow to the regime, short of killing the Tsar himself.* Plehve was the recognised symbol of reactionary policies and known to be a major influence over Nicolas II. The Emperor's response to his assassination would have the same effect as a statement of policy from the throne. The Tsar had in effect to choose whether to continue resisting public pressure, or to show that he now recognised that a gulf existed between his government and public opinion, however great the distance between the latter and the terrorists. He decided that it would be more expedient, in view of the course of the war, to be conciliatory. He appointed to succeed Plehve the moderate and well-meaning Governor of Vilna, Prince P. D. Svyatopolk-Mirsky, a man whose 'outstanding trait was a desire to remain at peace with everyone and live in an atmosphere of friendship'.[4] It was also hoped that his success with high Polish society would stand the regime in good stead in its present difficulties with the national minorities along the imperial periphery.

If Nicolas imagined that the mere act of appointing a 'nice' Minister of the Interior would immediately pacify the public he was to be gravely disillusioned. Svyatopolk-Mirsky was appointed as a man who, as he stated immediately upon taking up

---

* Azef and his chief, General Gerasimov, had a private agreement, by which Azef would do everything to prevent an attempt on the Tsar from succeeding, as long as the police left other leading Socialist Revolutionaries at large, thus saving Azef from falling under suspicion.[3]

his post, had confidence in society and in its institutions, and who expected to be approached by public figures with a view to active and constructive collaboration. He reinforced his words with a number of small but telling measures, designed to relieve public pressure. The liberals of the zemstvo movement were permitted to function again in the war effort, and those of its leaders who had suffered restrictions under Plehve were now released. Censorship of the press was eased, and police activities, except against the revolutionaries, slightly curbed. Public pressure was, however, in no way reduced. On the contrary the effect was to unleash a torrent of demands from the clubs and professional associations, the zemstvos, the universities, all urging that this new expression of confidence be crystallised by the introduction of representative government.

This campaign was organised by the Union of Liberation. True to his principles, Svyatopolk-Mirsky tried to prevail upon the Tsar to make concessions, but in view of the now blatant anti-government and anti-Tsarist character of vocal public opinion, Nicolas would not comply. So long as it had seemed that progressive leaders had wanted only to offer their help to the government in working out constitutional reforms, the Tsar could be persuaded to relax his grip. But now, late in 1904, when the call was for universal suffrage, a constituent assembly, and, by association, the abolition of the autocracy, Nicolas decided that enough had been given and that now the country must return to law and order.

He issued an Edict on 25 December 1904 in which he virtually did no more than reaffirm the intentions of his grandfather's reforms of the 1860s and 1870s. Thus the peasants would get their full rights, the zemstvos would be permitted to function on a slightly wider basis, the factory workers would be insured by the State, religious and ethnic minorities would be treated more fairly, and the press would be given clearer indications of the limits within which it might operate. In the meantime disorders would not be tolerated and meetings and manifestations, such as had been witnessed during late 1904, must cease forthwith.

Nicolas failed to realise that by now the public had developed an appetite for real changes in the nature of government and would readily respond to the slightest prompting to demand them.

As news reached the capital of the fall of Port Arthur, in December 1904, the population adjusted its mood of political despondency to one of tragic shock. But it was soon to be followed by an event which would galvanise public feeling to even greater depths. This event took place in the heart of the capital and seemed to reveal in one brief day more about the government's nervous defensiveness than all the news from the east. The event became known as 'Bloody Sunday', 22 January 1905.

The disaster came as a result of an organised labour demonstration on a scale which by far surpassed the efforts of any of the socialist parties, and was mainly the work of one man, Father Gapon—plus police support. 'Police socialism', under the inspiration of Zubatov, had been consumed in the fires of 1903, when Zubatovite strikes had led to a wave of unrest in the south of Russia which had got entirely out of police control. The backlash of their own zeal had led to the discredit of such enterprises and to the demotion of Zubatov; Grand Duke Sergei, an ardent supporter of the scheme, never again succumbed to similar temptations and Moscow, his domain, remained free of Zubatovism.

In St Petersburg, on the other hand, there was great concern among the police at the sheer proportions which labour manifestations and strikes could take. Control of the workers was the legitimate ideal of any police chief of the city. It was normal practice for the police to have their informants and agents working among the revolutionary organisations; similarly, they took steps to share control of the mass labour movement, inasmuch as control was feasible at all. Sudden moves of such large concentrations of angry workmen as there were in the capital were no less likely to produce spectacular and dangerous consequences than the assassination of a minister.

Early in 1904, with the approval of the Minister of the Interior, Plehve, the Petersburg police had succeeded in setting up the 'Assembly of Russian Workers' under the leadership of the priest Gapon. The purposes of the Assembly were ostensibly education and the improvement of working and leisure facilities. Like Zubatov, Gapon aimed at substituting positive ideas of self-improvement in the minds of the workers in place of the negative and destructive ones that were being planted there by the socialists. The most appealing argument which Gapon used was that only the state was sufficiently powerful and organised to protect the workers' interests against unjust exploitation by the bosses. Police protection of Gapon's movement, though it was covert, afforded two welcome luxuries to its members, first the economic and social benefits of clubs, tea-rooms, concerts, lectures—in a word the movement had money; secondly, it meant an end of the brutal treatment which workers on strike had come to expect and dread at the hands of the police and militia.

Charming and simple in his manner, Gapon succeeded in gaining the complete confidence of the Governor of St Petersburg. With his support he quickly established himself in a position of almost pontifical authority in his ever-growing parish and duly drew from this following still greater conviction of his unique destiny. His influence and prestige grew in rhythm with the nation's declining fortunes in the war, so that by the end of 1904 his organisation, with eleven branches in the capital, could count nearly 9,000 members, with a following perhaps ten times larger.[5]

The Assembly attracted a number of Social Democrats and Socialist Revolutionaries who successfully carried on political indoctrination of the workers, encouraging them to take up militant political demands in addition to their peaceful economic ones. Gapon, who was as much the expression of trends within his movement as its guide, found himself in harmony with the demands of the Union of Liberation by the end of 1904, a result of his own contacts with its leaders and the changes of mood inside his Assembly. But in his profound patriotism, religious belief, and love of Tsar, as well as his instinctive conviction of the bond between the masses and the Tsar, Gapon rejected the direct revolutionary path, and counted instead on the Tsar's wisdom and generosity.

Some employers were not, however, as confident of peaceful relations as Gapon seemed to be, and the enormous potential of the Assembly gave them cause for anxiety, soon to be fully justified. Thus with the socialists inside the Assembly prodding it towards action, and a high degree of distrust present in factory management, the least provocative step could lead to conflict. That step was taken in December 1904 when four Assembly workers were dismissed from the Putilov Works by an unpopular foreman. A petition demanding their reinstatement and the dismissal of the foreman was rejected by the firm, and on 16 January 1905 the entire labour force at Putilov's, numbering 12,500, came out on strike. From that moment the government's second experiment with controlled trade unionism began to build up a reaction, compared with which Zubatov's mistakes of 1903 seem paltry.

Within four days the strike was spread by Gapon and his aides, to almost 150 firms in the capital and involved nearly 90,000 workers. The economic demands of the strikers were blatantly inordinate and it was not doubted that they would be rejected. Something much more dramatic than mere bargaining with managers had to come out of this massive show of solidarity. The idea of presenting a petition direct to the Tsar, while it seemed somewhat out of character, fired the imaginations of the overwhelming majority. But the document, as it gradually evolved out of numerous meetings and mass debates, contained political demands which gave it rather the appearance of a party manifesto.

Though loyalty and patriotism pervaded the petition and the language in which it was composed was redolent of old-world peasant-clerical deference, yet it left no doubt that the masses expected the Tsar to grant major political concessions. In emotional language it complained that the masses had 'become beggars, overburdened . . . humiliated . . . treated as slaves'. A socialist hand became evident when the petition claimed that the workers would never be able to improve their lot so long as they, 'like the rest of the Russian people, had no human rights—no right to speak, think, assemble . . .'.

The Tsar, it went on, must save his people by coming close to them, by 'letting them rule together with him'. 'Russia is too great . . . to be governed by bureaucrats alone. Popular representation is essential. . . . [the Tsar should] immediately summon representatives . . . of all classes . . . including the workers. Capitalists, workers, bureaucrats, priests, doctors and teachers— let them all . . . choose their own representatives. . . . Order the election of a constituent assembly on the basis of universal, secret and equal suffrage.' There followed a detailed list of demands, beginning with amnesty and continuing through almost every point in the *Liberation* programme and much that came from the Socialist Revolutionaries and the Social Democrats. The petition closed with a final appeal: 'If You will so command and take an oath that these needs of ours will be satisfied You will make Russia happy and glorious, and Your name will be engraved forever in our hearts and in the hearts of our descendants. But if You will not so command and heed not our prayer, we will die here on the square, in front of Your palace. . . . For us . . . it is either freedom and happiness or the grave. Let our lives be a sacrifice for suffering Russia. We do not grudge it, but offer it willingly.'[6]

The plan was to move in mass procession from all parts of the city to the Winter Palace, and there, on their knees, to watch Gapon hand the appeal to the Tsar himself. On 8 January Gapon informed Svyatopolk-Mirsky of his intentions, but the minister, already having taken precautions to maintain order, did not convey to the Tsar any inkling of what was afoot. Instead he ordered Gapon's arrest, hoping thus to avert the mass demonstration. The chief of police, General Fullon, knew it was beyond his powers at that moment to carry out the order, so great and so emotional was the priest's following. Realising there was nothing they could do to stop the procession setting forth, the minister and his aides, never once trying to make contact with the movement's leaders, planned means of dealing with the event itself. Fully aware of the terrible consequences of bloodshed, they nonetheless decided that if the workers chose to ignore orders to disperse, and pressed on to the palace, in spite of warning shots, then the troops were to fire into the crowds.

On 22 January the workers set out from all points with their icons and portraits of the Tsar and Tsarina and, singing hymns, converged on the Palace Square. The government's orders were carried out: failure to disperse was met with rifle fire, and the terrified crowds, which included women and children, scattered, returning after the drama only to pick up their dead and wounded. Over 100 were killed and more than 300 were wounded. Many of them were among the more militant demonstrators who persisted in congregating on the Palace Square and nearby, after the main tributaries of the procession had dispersed and the majority had gone home. The attempts, rather belated and marginal, of Social Democrats and Socialist Revolutionaries to inject a note of violence and aggressiveness into the occasion were utterly frustrated by the disciplined action of the military.

The outrage turned a number of workers into active revolutionaries, liquidated finally all traces of 'police socialism', and provided massive ammunition to all shades of opposition opinion. Its most significant effect was to harden the strikers' resolution to continue the strike, not out of new-born hatred of the Tsar—most of them remained loyal, if hurt and confused—but because they had taken a major step along the path of their own emancipation and felt impelled to consolidate it. Still more important was the effect on the authorities, who were now anxious lest an enraged population demand payment for their savagery against peaceful workers.

News of 22 January spread throughout Russia and in every industrial centre was answered with fresh strikes, until in the course of January alone nearly half-a-million workers came out on strike. Socialist influence and control were negligible, and demands were universally economic, except in territories where non-Russian nationalities predominated and national political aspirations found expression in the general labour ferment. Public indignation at the events of 22 January had no need of artificial stimulation, for the barest account of what had happened was sufficient to shock. The government made no attempt at explanation, but left the field open to stories of wild exaggeration, with which the parties of the opposition further inflamed public opinion. Student and professional bodies made common cause with the strikers, emphasising the political needs of the population as the underlying cause of the present crisis. The academic profession was particularly vociferous, and a large body of Petersburg University staff, as well as a group from the Academy of Sciences, proclaimed the need for representative government as the only possible solution. Similar resolutions were adopted throughout the country in professional societies.

On 17 February the Socialist Revolutionaries assassinated Grand Duke Sergei, the Tsar's uncle and a well-known extremist of the right. In response to this, and to the mounting chaos, the Tsar issued two acts, one sternly condemning all disruptive action and calling upon the Russian people to stand firm behind the throne; the other ordering his ministers to examine proposals being voiced in public for the reform of government. On the same day, 18 February, he published still another act, ordering his new Minister of the Interior, Bulygin,* to prepare the way for gathering 'worthy men, enjoying the confidence of the people, and elected by the people, to take part in the preliminary examination and consideration of legislative proposals'. At last the public demand for representative government had been conceded, though no mention had yet been made of the means whereby the people were to express themselves; nothing about elections or.parties had yet been said. Still, opposition opinion felt victorious rather than appeased. The Tsar's magnanimity was

* Svyatopolk-Mirsky was relieved of his post after Bloody Sunday.

interpreted as a retreat and the result was an outburst of political organisation and what was virtually electioneering.

Pre-eminent in these activities was the Union of Liberation which, having inspired the formation of various professional associations, coordinated them in May into one Union of Unions under the chairmanship of Paul Milyukov. Already the spokesman for the major part of the zemstvo constitutionalist movement, *Liberation*, now with a large socialist following in these specialist unions, became the spearhead of political sentiment extending over the entire field of opposition. Since this field was in reality a battleground, of strikes, peasant disorders, terrorist outrages and demonstrations, the Union of Liberation was in an ambiguous position, for the aims of the revolutionary movement, which began with overthrow of the regime, and those of the constitutionalists, who sought representative government, were incompatible in practice.

The implications of this united front were as yet unimagined by the liberals in tenuous command of it, for in the summer months of 1905 attention was focussed upon 'liberal' issues: the scope of the franchise, the alignment of parties and their programmes, but above all the advent of a constituent assembly, or representative government, as the culmination of the struggle for emancipation which had lasted for nearly a century.

Leaving aside for a moment the construction which organised socialists put on the situation, it is important to consider what understanding the masses had of these unfamiliar political events. When the workers and peasants rallied to the *Liberation* banner and shouted for a share in government, they were in reality merely extending their demands for better social and economic conditions from their bosses to the government, to society or to the world in general. They were letting their grievances become known. Their angry outbursts and their violence were not calculated to seize the political initiative, (precisely as some socialists feared), but were a lever for exacting attention and positive action from 'the authorities'. It would eventually emerge that the demand for political representation was easier to satisfy than demands for social and economic changes.

Throughout the summer of 1905 the Tsar and his ministers contemplated the mounting disorder, the spread of the strike movement, the multiplication of peasant violence, the public's intense disappointment with the defeats in the Far East. The political slogans and demands of all sectors of opinion echoed about them. Finally, in August, having started peace negotiations with Japan, the Tsar consented to the convocation of a State Duma, to take place by January 1906, and thus he set the seal on his promise of February 1905.

But what as far back as February had already seemed a meagre concession now, in August, seemed absurd. The majority of opposition opinion could not be expected to be satisfied with a franchise based on property qualifications and nationality, nor with an indirect electoral system that would ensure control by elements which only the government regarded as 'responsible'. It was plain that, with the war out of his way, Nicolas was going to reclaim the initiative. He was hoping to pacify the opposition by letting it play the parliamentary game so precious to it, but he would ensure that this interference in State affairs could not go beyond ineffective intellectual debate.

The declaration on the State Duma led to a split in the liberal ranks. The moderates wanted to accept the Duma, to take part in elections to it, and to work for the peaceful and legal implementations of reforms. The radicals were loth to relinquish the freedom of tactics which their illegal status permitted them, and which participation in the Duma would immediately curtail. They opted therefore to boycott the elections and to continue their campaign for a constituent assembly, elected by universal, direct, secret and equal suffrage.

The socialist parties had less difficulty in reaching a policy towards the Duma. Implacably opposed to any measure which would relieve the pressure against the regime and thus enable the autocracy to repair its defences against the revolution, the socialists attacked the government's offer of a Duma and called for its boycott. The class bias, embodied in the property quali-fications for the franchise, provided the chief target of socialist attacks. In September the Jewish *Bund* organised a conference in Riga, attended by the Bolsheviks and Mensheviks, and Polish, Ukrainian and Lettish Social Democrats. The high degree of militancy and sense of imminent success then prevalent among the organisations of the national minorities, was echoed by the vehemence of the conference. It declared for boycott and a general strike to disrupt the elections, followed by a general armed uprising and the democratic revolution.

The Mensheviks, no less revolutionary or militant than other groups, put forward a policy which was distinctive for its practicability, its socialist and democratic tone, and for the fact that it was entirely out of harmony with the conference as a whole. Akselrod, reiterating one of his most cherished notions, proposed that parallel elections should be held for the workers' own deputies. They would form assemblies which would be represented in a national 'people's' congress, as a counterpart to the State Duma. This proposal was an answer to the dis-franchisement which the Tsar's 'concession' implied, and it directly foreshadowed the emergence of workers' soviets and, in 1917, the Congress of Soviets. In their attitude to the Duma elections the Mensheviks also differed from the rest of socialist opinion, for they advocated using the elections as a platform for their views and for the further widespread, open agitation of the electorate against the regime.

But beyond declaiming upon the urgent need for an armed uprising, none of the socialist organisations could contribute much towards making it a reality, although their influence in the strikes that were to come would prove important. A new strike wave broke out in Moscow on 2 October when a union of printers, led by Menshevik supporters, came out on strike over a minor wage dispute. In no time the strike spread throughout a wide range of trades and industries in the city. Street demonstrators clashed with troops and police. Shots were fired by both sides (though where the strikers got firearms from is not known) and it seemed that Bloody Sunday was about to be re-enacted. The union leaders attempted to coordinate the movement and inflate it into a general political strike, but by the middle of October the spirit had gone out of the men and they were beginning to go back to work.

But only a week later, students and workers, joined by office-workers, created a purely political demonstration, proclaiming slogans of both *Liberation* and the revolutionary movement. Moscow railway workers, who were the most widely organised sector of the labouring population, were becoming impatient of negotiations being carried on by their union with the Ministry of Finance, which employed them, and were agitating for strike action. On 21 October they gave way to their impatience. In two days the Moscow railway system was brought to a halt, with the workers demanding, in addition to their economic programme, a constituent assembly and an amnesty for political prisoners. From the Moscow hub the strike radiated along the telegraph and railway systems, until by mid-October the entire railway system from the Baltic to Manchuria was at a standstill. Simultaneously, industries throughout the country slowed down and stopped either from lack of supplies or local strike action, or both. Russia was in the grip of a general strike.

The strike very rapidly lost the appearance of a labour protest and acquired that of general political demonstration. A near-insurrectionary situation was barely averted in Kharkov, when workers and students held the university against troops and had to be assured a safe conduct as the alternative to open battle. A similar occurrence took place in Moscow. Such incidents, though not common, contributed greatly to the highly charged atmosphere. The October general strike became the opportunity for almost everybody to express a desire for change, though there was great disparity of opinion as to the extent this change should reach. Thus, august academicians 'came out' and joined liberal professors and lawyers; teachers and doctors expressed their solidarity with the factory workers, and even State Senators, like many other members of the administration, made token gestures in favour of change. The fact that such diverse elements of Russian society united in their demand for change imparted to this general strike the character of revolution.

Socialist influence in the strikes was considerable and was directed towards two ends: first, to maintain the militancy of the strike until the government surrendered; secondly, to safeguard the popularity of the strike. With varying success local strike committees, some with socialist leaders, some without, turned into local organs of self-government, supervising food supplies and strike funds. In the capital one such strike committee rapidly grew in size and influence, and on 26 October constituted itself the St Petersburg Soviet of Workers' Deputies. Its chairman was a Menshevik lawyer, Khrustalev-Nosar, but it was the vice-chairman, Leon Trotsky, who achieved fame and notoriety both for himself and for the Soviet, with his inflammatory and incisive speeches, delivered before thousands in a ringing, martial voice.

A prominent Social Democrat, neither Bolshevik nor Menshevik, Trotsky's non-factional party status added to his qualifications for the role he found so congenial, that of tribune of the masses. For in spite of the great proportion of Mensheviks among its leaders, the Soviet, like other soviets which sprang up throughout the provinces, expressed no party line, but rather acted upon any issue or opportunity to keep the temper of the workers generally revolutionary. To this extent it is legitimate to describe the soviet movement as 'Menshevik', as it harmonised more closely with the Menshevik doctrine of mass, spontaneous action, than it did with Lenin's insistence on the control and manipulation of the mass movement through a compact élite.

Four days after the formation of the Petersburg Soviet, though quite unconnected with it, the Tsar was prevailed upon to make a major concession for civil peace. On 30 October he issued a Manifesto in which he promised civil rights, including freedom of speech, conscience, assembly and association, and inviolability of the person; a broad franchise for elections to the Duma, and the prospect of ultimate universal suffrage; and representa-

tive government. The Tsar took this course to the accompaniment of dire warnings from his counsellors that the alternative
would be civil war and threats to the throne, which only a
military dictatorship and the severest repression of the population
would be able to avert. His chief counsellor at this time was
Sergei Witte, whose approach, beliefs and indeed person,
Nicolas had always found objectionable. But Witte had just
brought off a peace with Japan, at Portsmouth, USA, which was
less onerous than might have been anticipated, and he was
enjoying the reputation of a conquering hero. Thus it was that
Nicolas was prepared to let him exploit his popularity to achieve
a second peace, at home, while for his part Witte was more than
willing to serve his emperor under conditions which amounted to
his complete mastery of state affairs.

The Tsar's apparent capitulation acted as a stimulus to further
revolutionary unrest throughout the country. An amnesty,
decreed a week after the Manifesto, became the lever for creating
local disruption, with strikers and agitators openly inciting the
crowds to take possession of the gaols and to free the inmates.
Mutinies followed in the navy and the army, triggered by revolutionary agitation and by impatience for demobilisation and the
return home. Peasant uprisings multiplied; workers' soviets came
into being in emulation of Petersburg; the national minorities
broke out violently against Russian domination.

Right-wing and court circles, who had always hated Witte,
both for himself and for his over-zealous westernising, now
regarded him as a traitor for urging the concessions upon the
Tsar. It was known that Witte had argued that political concessions would make it easier for him to negotiate with western
Jewish bankers the enormous loans that Russia needed to pay for
the war loss. It could thus be said that the Tsar was forced to sell
out to Jews, a proposition of the utmost repugnance to Russian
reactionary opinion. The police and newspapers of the proto-
fascist organisations, the Black Hundreds, which enjoyed support
in the highest circles, combined to create a series of pogroms

against the Jews. They began the week after the Tsar's Manifesto appeared, and were more or less intense throughout the following two-year period during which the government was busy crushing the revolutionaries. The large number of Jews among the most prominent revolutionaries, among the radical liberals, and among owners and editors of progressive newspapers, provided an excuse for government and private right-wing organisations to terrorise dissident opinion, and at the same time furnish an outlet for the inflamed mood of the mob. The democratic component in the Manifesto was neutralised by the government's persistent unwillingness to condemn publicly and outright Great Russian chauvinism.

Witte was empowered to form a new cabinet, whose composition would satisfy the clamour for popular, or congenial government, while at the same time ensuring loyalty to the throne. Witte sent for Dmitri Shipov, the moderate leader of the zemstvo-constitutionalist movement, and together they compiled a list of possible ministers, among whom were prominent men of known constitutionalist views. Witte had no objection to these candidates but made it a condition that they should demonstrate a serious approach to matters of state and openly acknowledge the need to uphold law and order in the country.[7] This proviso was aimed at excluding pure intellectuals and allies of the revolutionaries.

But, by October 1905, Shipov and his close friends were a minority in their own movement and their usefulness to Witte was limited to the influence they could exert upon the more radical majority. Regrettably for the Shipov–Witte talks, the leaders of this majority had their own conditions for entering the cabinet. These were put to Witte by F. Kokoshkin, a radical intellectual well versed in constitutional law.

The liberals' choice of this uncompromising spokesman indicated a lack of realism on their part.[8] The condition put by Kokoshkin to Witte, was the convocation of a constituent assembly which would frame a constitution, in other words the *Liberation* programme. The events of 1905 had amply demonstrated how widely this programme was supported in the country, and since the government had turned to the leaders of the constitutional movement, it seemed reasonable to the liberals to make this demand the basis of their negotiations. But the liberals certainly knew that their demands were in excess of the Tsar's concessions, and were in fact the anticipation of the work to be done by the coming Duma. It was plain that they were pressing an advantage and keeping up the pressure. Opposition had evidently become a habit, and it seems that the opportunity to share in government, the cherished goal of generations, was as repellent to the liberals as the impulse to oppose government was attractive to them.

But, if the liberal vanguard of public opinion was too fastidious to accept a share of power, it is also true that the circumstances of the offer and the style of the would-be donor, Witte, did nothing to allay qualms. Witte held the crude view that a government that would strongly suppress disorder and be simultaneously enlightened and reforming, should consist of a harsh minister of the interior and a liberal minister of justice. He did not appreciate the main point of all the public protest of 1905, which was aimed at producing a change of outlook in the government as a whole. His departmental approach was out of harmony with even the mildest moderates and did much to foster suspicion. Trotsky succinctly expressed opposition feeling: 'Is not the hangman Trepov [Governor-General of the capital] the undisputed master of Petersburg? . . . The Tsar's Manifesto . . . is only a scrap of paper. . . . Today it has been given to us and tomorrow it will be taken away and torn in pieces . . . this paper liberty. . . .'[9]

With the appointment of the known reactionary, P. N. Durnovo, as Minister of the Interior, the greater part of the public began uneasily to share this doubt: *plus ça change, plus c'est la même chose*. However much they may have deplored and feared the continued violence and disorder which the Manifesto did nothing to curb, the public was equally dismayed by the government's rapid resort to habitual means for dealing with the situation. It was widely suspected and easily believed that the pogroms launched a week after the Tsar's capitulation were condoned and aided by government officials and the police, and that they were to serve as a demonstration of loyalty to the 'truly Russian' ideals of Autocracy, Orthodoxy and Great Russian Nationality. The government's virtual silence and inactivity on this score only confirmed its complicity. Violence and illegality at both ends of the political spectrum made it almost impossible for responsible public opinion to accept that a new era of peaceful reconstruction was about to begin.

This doubt was reinforced by Witte's new cabinet, which, having failed in his attempts to attract public men of the opposition into it, Witte had had to create out of existing administrators. Although some of them were relatively progressive in their views the impression of an old regime government was inescapable. The political deadlock between government and society was now complete. Both sides in the conflict believed their point of view vindicated by this failure to reach common ground. The constitutionalists claimed that they had upheld the tradition of public service, unhampered by bureaucratic obstructionism. They pointed out that their political demands had emerged in the course of their zemstvo work, that only a share of power could solve some of the problems they came up against in that work. Though this was true enough, the wider truth was that the zemstvo movement was the product of a political struggle of long standing and that the zemstvo had re-emerged as the vehicle of that struggle in a later context.

What, then, lay at the root of the government's contradictory behaviour? The Tsar and most of his ministers believed that all talk of political reform and concessions, even moderate, was the thoughtless and dangerous chatter of intellectuals. Western notions of democracy and representative government were, they believed, alien to the Russian People, who without a strong paternalistic government would fall into anarchy and violence. The release of such elemental force would threaten the entire system. In this alarming analysis the only point which proved to have some validity was the last: once the masses were moved to make inordinate demands in a violent manner the system, like any other, was indeed threatened. It was, however, as much the mistake of the opposition as of the government to suppose that this hazard was peculiarly Russian, and that it embodied the essence of the Russian polity. This spectre of the omnipotence of the Russian folk served to justify the inertia and fear of change which dominated the government. It also helps to explain their ineptitude in dealing with articulate political opinion.

The impact of events in October led to the permanent division of the zemstvo–constitutionalist movement into its liberal and moderate components. The majority, led by P. N. Milyukov, formed the Constitutional Democratic Party (Kadet, from its Russian initials KD) on the platform of the Union of Liberation, and the moderate minority led by Shipov organised their own party, based on acceptance of the October Manifesto. For the latter the Tsar's statement was the culmination of the political struggle of the nineteenth century, and now the national interest could best be served by working for the implementation of the Tsar's promises in such peaceful cooperation as the government would allow. The party was known variously as the Party of Peaceful Reconstruction, and the Union of October 17.* As for the zemstvos, which had provided so much of the striking force of the old emancipation movement, they now returned to their proper tasks, leaving the national political arena to those who had fought to enter it.

By the end of the year the formation of political parties, for the first time permitted in Russia, would channel liberal opinion away from the revolutionary movement. The strike movement would lose its vigour, although Moscow would see one final convulsion. The government under Witte's lead would regain its confidence and stability, and would be on the way to re-establishing its mastery.

* This was the date of the October Manifesto, Old Style.

5

Revolutionaries in Revolution

The turbulence of events in Russia was matched by the violence
of the Social Democrats' factional feud. Martov persisted in his
refusal to participate in the new editorial board of *Iskra*, and
Plekhanov, in lonely partnership with Lenin, could not long stand
the isolation from his colleagues of twenty-five years' standing,
Akselrod and Zasulich. He quickly found an opportunity to
propose their reinstatement, and this provoked Lenin's resignation. This was an act entirely out of character for Lenin and he
would never again relinquish an office or title so charged with
party authority. Lenin seems to have been more hurt by his
quarrel with Martov than his loss of party office, for Martov
was one of his rare comrades for whom Lenin felt an affection
transcending political consideration. When Lenin was on his
death bed in 1923 he commented sadly: 'they say that Martov
is about to die. Is that true?'[1]

The Bolshevik–Menshevik dichotomy developed with increasing clarity not least because, a personal split having taken
place, it was incumbent upon the antagonists to provide 'scientific' explanations. The definition coined by Lenin in his own
painstaking analysis of the congress was that Bolsheviks were
'hard' Iskraists, while Mensheviks were 'soft'. The implication was
that, while he and his followers were unflinching in the struggle
against heterodoxy in doctrine and plurality in organisation,

Martov and his supporters in *Iskra* were vacillating and allowed sentiment and personalities to cloud their political judgement.

While the rival ideologies were taking shape, the Social Democrats at home in the underground carried on as usual. In many cases it was weeks, if at all, before 'delegations' reported back to their committees on the results of their travels abroad, and in general the effect was to produce bewilderment and exasperation. Local organisers, busy enough trying to create and maintain the semblance of coherent political activity were reluctant, even if able, to introduce doctrinal subtlety into their work. They were already facing great difficulty in delineating the aims of Social Democracy amid encroachments and blandishments by the dynamic liberal movement. To have, in addition, to declare for Bolshevism or Menshevism, and to explain the choice to the rank and file, came as a diversion, redolent of émigré squabbles and politicking, and was a task totally alien to the business-like attitudes of the underground 'professionals'. Besides, most full-time revolutionaries inside Russia saw their function as much in fulfilling a *social* need for the working class, as in representing a political party.

The haziness of allegiances and demarcation that had existed before the split, and through which *Iskra*'s compaign had cut an arbitrary swathe, continued in spite of the new situation. Many committees harboured both factions, a fact which was formalised in the North-West provinces by the establishment of 'joint' committees. This state of affairs arose partly out of a need to nourish all available resources: the seduction of the revolutionary movement by the radical wing of the liberal constitutionalists was gaining momentum. But haziness over the split also flowed from the artificiality inherent in the quarrel, at least in the eyes of local organisers. If, as the Mensheviks complained, Lenin put all his trust in the clandestine nucleus of professional revolutionaries and looked with distrust on the workers' own efforts, then there was little that local organisers could find wrong in such an attitude. To them the integrity of the 'organisation' was an article of faith, and a condition of survival.

On the other hand, they could sympathise with the Menshevik denunciation of Lenin's uncompromising demand for total control of local affairs by the Central Committee. 'Organisational democratism', or local autonomy, appealed to provincial organisers, but it decisively undermined the notion of a Menshevik wing as a coherent group.

Lenin's rigid centralism alienated most of his erstwhile comrades and would continue to repel new party workers. But his unswerving devotion to that principle in the long run served him better than democratic toleration served his opponents, for it meant that he could eventually claim the loyalty of a number, however small, of personally dedicated followers. Menshevism, on the other hand, remained essentially anarchical in that no single leader or leadership ever wielded power and party authority in its name.

Yet this 'minorityism' attracted the great majority of the best organisers, thinkers, speakers, and most of the long-standing party members. Essentially they were bound by little more than their common rejection of Lenin and their wish for freedom of thought and expression. The cost of this freedom was a wide range of ideas on tactics and aims, which deprived the Menshevik wing of the one vital weapon needed by a revolutionary party in a revolutionary situation: one loud voice uttering one simple message. *Iskra*, under the Mensheviks, became more an intellectuals' debating journal than a 'spark to kindle a flame'. Official editorial policy, formulated by Martov and Dan, vied with cautionary exhortations from Plekhanov and Akselrod to the right, and extremist ideas from Trotsky to the left.[2] If any single tenet was shared by these divergent schools it was that the Russian working class could and would develop its political life along lines similar to those which had guided the German workers towards the great Social Democratic Party of Germany. Thus Menshevism perpetuated itself in Russia rather as a 'tendency' than as a party.

The Bolsheviks were not at the opposite pole to the Mensheviks on the spectrum of Russian socialism, but were rather of another species. For if Mensheviks devoted themselves to the tasks of facilitating the progress of the proletariat towards political power in the state, the Leninists never lost sight of their goal, which was to facilitate their *own* progress to power by means, and in the name, of the proletariat.

Lenin's reputation as a narrow factionalist continued to stick to him, in spite of the fact that leading Mensheviks were equally reluctant to rejoin forces. The two wings were genuinely irreconcilable, for the Mensheviks constantly anticipated Lenin's lapses into stubbornness and dictatorship, and Lenin could never relinquish his own characterisation of them as opportunists, compromisers—'softs'. Though it was some years before the two parties came to formal recognition of the split, it was virtually final in 1903.

The significance of Russian Social Democracy in the years 1903–5 dwindles sharply when set against the general background of social and political events. Some strikes and demonstrations of notable proportions were the work of Social Democrats. Some thousands of workers were organised party members. And many zemstvo workers, intellectuals, professionals, could be counted as Social Democrats. But even for them it was not the Social Democratic leaders who provided the political interest of the day. With growing momentum the left wing of the liberal, constitutional democratic movement was gathering force and mustering hope among the restive masses. It would indeed be surprising if the Social Democrats had been more effective in Russia, since the entire leadership of both factions was still abroad in exile, and the local committees could do little more than drift along in habitual ways, confused by contradictory exhortations from abroad, in what was becoming a hotbed of revolution. It is indeed a cliché in the histories of the party that 1905 (like February 1917) took it by surprise.

During almost the whole of 1904 Lenin's energies were consumed in feuding with the Mensheviks, a campaign of violent self-justification. In letters and articles he harangued himself into a state of nervous exhaustion, so that in the summer Krupskaya had to take him off to the mountains for a complete change. Rested and more relaxed, he returned to Switzerland in the late summer to rally his forces.

With the heightening of revolutionary temper in Russia some of the most militant socialist intellectuals were attracted by Lenin's dynamism. Not one of them would remain constant to him, nor render to him the kind of blind allegiance which, in his eyes, constituted comradeship. In due course they would assert themselves against Lenin's line, only to return to him when his views seemed once again to coincide with their 'Bolshevik' mood.

What Lenin constantly sought in his followers was the committed *agent*; they need not be ideologically committed, indeed Lenin even admitted that there could be open differences of conviction which need not be crucial. What mattered was perfect control by the centre over the organisation in practical matters. In other words Lenin's line was not to be questioned and agents must suffer personal conflicts of principle with clenched teeth. Essentially, Lenin's agents had to be Leninists, rather than Bolsheviks, for while a Bolshevik was a man with certain beliefs, a Leninist was a man who served Lenin. At times the two would merge, as in 1904–7, and in 1917. And again, they would bifurcate, in times of debate rather than action, as in the Stolypin era and in the early years of the Soviet regime after the civil war.

The intellectuals who gave Lenin powerful literary support were nowhere near as numerous as those who wrote for the Mensheviks. His team included the Marxist philosopher Bogdanov; the journalist and future Soviet Commissar of education, Lunacharsky; and Vorovsky, the future diplomat, as well as some of the most practised underground workers in the party, including Leonid Krasin and G. Krzhizhanovsky.

With these forces, and some local support in Russia, Lenin set about reconstituting his own organisation, not as a faction of the party, but as the party itself. Now that *Iskra* was totally Menshevik it was of first importance to Lenin that he establish his own paper to vie with his opponents for the attention and allegiance of the party workers in Russia. He chose to call it *Vpered* (*Forward*), an indication that he would spend no more time lamenting the loss of prestige and continuity with the past, which his departure from *Iskra* had entailed. Now his first concern was to carry on the struggle by means of 'the most varied and widespread agitation, by the spoken and written word'.[3] *Vpered* began to appear in December 1904.

His second task was to convoke a new party congress. The pattern of the campaign was precisely what it has been for the Second Congress: first a powerful propaganda campaign through a dynamic newspaper, followed by the party congress, which would set an official stamp on the works of the organisation. He published pamphlets and leaflets as though his membership of the party Central Committee entitled him to act in its name but without its sanction; his actions were a repudiation of the existing and recognised organs and institutions of the party. His campaign for a new party congress, based as it was on very slender support, had the purpose of mustering a Bolshevik assembly under the party's auspices, thus expropriating the party title from its present Menshevik holders.

Feelings about the split among leading party members can be judged by the fact that the Central Committee, though composed of Bolsheviks, was in general inclined towards peaceful co-existence with the Mensheviks. It is true that this attitude derived largely from the weakness of their position: the Central Organ (*Iskra*) with all its facilities and funds was in Menshevik hands. In spite of this, and in spite of Lenin's constant nagging at it to be more anti-Menshevik, the Central Committee managed to carry out its functions.

Though he had far less external support than his opponents, Lenin had the major advantage over them that his whole approach was based on offensive strategy. He recognised the importance of an official title. He had recognised it in 1902, when he created an 'Organisational Committee' to convene the Second Party Congress, and he repeated his experience in 1904, by creating a 'Bureau of Committees of the Party Majority' (playing on the word 'majority'—*Bolshinstvo–Bolshevik*) and by making its declared purpose the campaign for the 'Third Party Congress'.

All the central institutions of the party were opposed to Lenin's plan for a congress and he was even expelled from the Central Committee for persisting. The situation changed unexpectedly in his favour in February 1905, when nine out of the eleven Central Committee members were suddenly arrested in Russia. It was plain to the two remaining members that only a congress could restore adequate authority to any newly formed committee. But the Mensheviks, who controlled the party's highest office, the Council, still remained indignantly aloof from this new venture of Lenin's, and merely satisfied themselves with statements to the effect that the Bolshevik gathering was unconstitutional and irrelevant to the party as a whole.

In April 1905 Lenin opened his 'Third Congress of the RSDRP' in London. Even he admitted its unrepresentative nature, there being less than the quorum which the Central Committee had undertaken to recognise. Some delegates were uneasy. They allowed themselves, however, to be persuaded, by Lenin and other enthusiastic delegates, that their presence more than compensated for the absence of others, and that this meeting was therefore all the more representative of the genuinely revolutionary wing of Russian Social Democracy.

Among some of the delegates Lenin encountered resistance to his intention to break for good with the Mensheviks and to go ahead with his plans for a purely Bolshevik party. In fact, many of them had come to his congress under the impression that its purpose was rather to reunite the party. His own propaganda was responsible for this misapprehension, for he had based his campaign for a new congress on the need to rally forces in the revolutionary situation in Russia. The delegates now realised that Lenin's calls for the preparation of an armed uprising under the party's leadership, which had much appeal among the militants in the Bolshevik underground, concealed a matter which was more precious to him, namely, the struggle for control of the official party.

Lenin was forced to compromise and to allow a resolution calling for steps to be taken to bring about reunion on the basis of Menshevik recognition of the new Central Committee and the Third Congress. The congress wished to create the impression that its purposes were conciliatory. The tactics decided upon, and kept secret from the rest of the party, were 'old-Iskraist': where a Menshevik committee refused to submit to the new party authority (i.e. Bolshevik Central Committee), a Bolshevik organisation would be formed in rivalry, the existing committee would be declared defunct, and the Bolshevik committee would be 'legitimised'.

A Menshevik conference was held in Geneva at about the same time as Lenin's. Its proceedings illustrate much of what distinguished the two factions. First, the delegates recognised their inadequacy as representatives of the entire party, and so satisfied themselves with the title of a 'conference'. Their disclaimer was also meant to help towards reunification with the Bolsheviks. Similarly, they did nothing to challenge the legitimacy of the new Bolshevik Central Committee, but on the contrary gave it *de facto* confirmation by forming their own central committee under the ambiguous and ephemeral name of 'Organising Committee'.[4] Thus in terms of party authority they positively smoothed Lenin's path. Plekhanov, who had urged the conference to adopt a fighting attitude towards Lenin's illegal activities, resigned from the *Iskra* editorial board in protest against so much appeasement. In spite of what they knew of Lenin and his methods, the Mensheviks used their conference to declare their abdication from party authority, in the name of reunification. They disarmed themselves in the forced belief that Lenin would work for unity.

The Mensheviks were vulnerable on one crucial point—lack of a leader with compelling authority equal to Lenin's. Whatever injuries and setbacks the Bolsheviks suffered, and they would be many, their continued functioning as a revolutionary party was always ensured by the existence of their leader Lenin. The resolutions adopted by the Mensheviks at their conference were not noticeably less revolutionary than the Bolsheviks', and they had the advantage in Russian conditions of 1905 that they encompassed mass action more imaginatively than their rivals. But in their present powerless position their resolutions were unauthorised and, more important, their 'democratic' attitude to the local committees was an open invitation to Bolshevik enterprise.

The rush of events taking place inside Russia made all attempts to demarcate Social Democratic organisations—to say nothing of the non-party supporters who constituted the driving force of the revolutionary movement—ineffective. The socialist parties and factions became during 1905 an undifferentiated chorus, barely discernible above the general tumult. More than that, when local Social Democrats made attempts to make the Petersburg Soviet a party organisation they were rebuffed by the rank and file of the Soviet and had to remain content with its non-party nature.

Though the Soviet was nominally non-party it was evident that its leadership was heavily Menshevik. This was true in spite of the fact that Trotsky, its star performer, was neither Menshevik nor Bolshevik. The Soviet's independence from party controls and the predominance of Mensheviks in it were two factors which at first made local Bolsheviks wary of becoming involved. Lenin's first reaction to the formation of the Soviet was positive. Right up to the moment when he heard of its existence, Lenin had consistently attacked Menshevik ideas of mass non-party organisations. Akselrod's dream of a workers' congress, a revolutionary self-government, was a major target for Lenin's attacks, even at the time the Soviet was formed.[5] Now that the fact was accomplished, however, Lenin's revolutionary zeal—from afar—and his determination to be at the heart of events overcame his partisan bias, and he became enthusiastic over this 'potential revolutionary government'.[6]

At the same time he wrote to Plekhanov lengthily that the situation in Russia, and the legal existence of a party organ (*Novaya Zhizn*) in the capital, were pressing evidence that the exiled leaders should return home and unite their forces. The proposal was a personal one to Plekhanov, rather than a general call for unity to all Mensheviks, and the letter was private.[7] Nonetheless it was an indication that at the time of his return to Russia Lenin was contemplating an alliance of a kind, which a year before would have caused him sleepless nights. In Stockholm, en route to Petersburg, he exulted over events at home and expanded on his thoughts in a letter* to the Bolshevik newspaper *Novaya Zhizn* (*New Life*).

The chief burden of this long letter was that the Social Democrats at home must check their impulse to attach the Soviet to the party. Its great value, Lenin asserted, was precisely that it embodied the aggressive alliance of Social Democrats and revolutionary bourgeois democrats that the party had always advocated. It should be noted here that the 'revolutionary bourgeois democrats' in this context were the Socialist Revolutionaries in the Soviet. Lenin urged the Social Democrats to overlook the theoretical inconsistencies and non-socialist views of the Socialist Revolutionaries, for 'it would be absurd and madness to expel dedicated and honest revolutionary democrats at a such a moment'. As for their inconsistencies, 'we'll settle all that without difficulty because our ideas are corroborated by history itself... If our little book (*What is to be Done?*) has not taught them social-democracy, then our revolution will.'[8]

Lenin spoke of the Soviet as a potential revolutionary government, and he exhorted it so to proclaim itself. He castigated Social Democrats for their criticism of the Soviet's broad base and declared that it was not yet broad enough. The Soviet must attract deputies from among the sailors and soldiers, from the revolutionary peasants and from the revolutionary intelligentsia. For the present situation at home, as it seemed to him from 'the inadequate paper facts' at his disposal, all efforts should be directed towards rallying a massive armed attack against the regime. To the 'combat unit' of the Bolshevik committee in Petersburg he had written, on 16 October, 'I am horrified, I

---

* It was not published until 1940.

swear it, horrified to think that you've been talking about bombs for *over half a year*, and still you haven't made one!'[9]

He had been studying the art of armed insurrection during the summer and, right up to his return to Russia on 8 November seems to have been preparing for some real action. It was not long after his return, however, that Lenin's 'mass-action' mood gave way to his customary obsession with party and factional matters, and he took up instead the issue of party unity. This was probably the result of his realisation that Trotsky's position in the Soviet was paramount and that the revolutionary strike movement was not the well-organised army that he had imagined it to be.

Lenin would have no part in any undertaking which he did not himself totally control. He rationalised his withdrawal on the grounds that the Soviet's non-party character compromised it as a revolutionary force; and he now believed it to be merely a workers' organisation run by the bourgeoisie and its leaders in the Union of Liberation. Once having recognised that there was no place for himself within the scope of the Soviet's activities, he concentrated his efforts elsewhere. There was no question of making a party issue out of the general situation, for to do so would have exposed him to renewed attacks of sectarian obstructionism. Instead he reserved his utterances on the subject to mild reminders to party workers of their more basic loyalty, but otherwise he did not interfere in their taking part in the work of soviets, in the capital or elsewhere.

Trotsky's triumphant policy of non-partisan leadership of the Soviet was hardly more palatable to the Menshevik leaders than it was to Lenin, but they could at least draw comfort from the patent fact that the Soviet's outlook and prospects were harmonious with their policies. Of greater importance was the fact that, paradoxically, it was during this non-partisan era of mass, soviet action that more and more workers found their way into the party organisations, oblivious or indifferent to the factional strife. Combined with the spontaneous tendency of party organisers in the provinces to combine whatever forces presented themselves

and form committees of the RSDRP, neither Bolshevik nor
Menshevik, this infusion of fresh blood into the party offered the
leaders an opportunity to recapture some of the initiative among
the workers.

The cry now was to sink past differences and to convene a
unification congress, at which new party principles embodying a
democratic approach to organisation should be proclaimed.
Lenin shared a view prevalent among socialist leaders that the
main conflict with Tsarism was round the corner and with this
in mind, he too campaigned for a 'Fourth Congress'. Reiterating the ideas he had formulated in *What is to be Done?* he proposed that the party should at all costs retain and protect its
clandestine central apparatus, and that all efforts should be made
to recruit and create more and more new, overt and covert,
partisan and sympathetic organisations.[10] What he did not make
known to those with whom he was proposing unity, was that he
had every intention of preserving his own clandestine apparatus.
It was the essential difference between Bolsheviks and Mensheviks that the latter took no similar precautions.

Before the Unification Congress took place, its chief aims were
overtaken by events in Russia. By mid-December 1905 the
enthusiasm of the strikers in Petersburg was flagging, and the
leaders of the Soviet were faced with the choice of either sus-
taining the strike, or adopting new and wider tactics. At that time
Trotsky's partner in the Soviet was Alexander Helphand, known
as Parvus, one of the most intriguing figures in the entire revolutionary movement, literally and metaphorically. He claimed to
have originated all the movement's best ideas, ideas which others
peeled off him like skins off an onion, as he once said in a deprived
mood. His idea in December 1905 was to declare a general withdrawal of all savings in gold, and a refusal to pay taxes. This, he
claimed on the basis of his study of the government's financial
situation, would bring down Witte's regime in a trice. In spite
of prompt action by the government, the value of Russian stock
fell on foreign markets. But the government now had the pretext
it needed to put an end to the Soviet altogether. On 16 December,

the day after the boycott had been passed by the Soviet, the entire assembly of 190 deputies was arrested.

With the end of the Soviet the strike also died out, without a single outcry from the masses against the summary 'old-regime' treatment of their cherished spokesmen. The workers had little heart left to respond to a final call from the Social Democrats for a renewal of the general strike. Petersburg's labour population at last quietened down after a whole year passed largely in a state of penurious agitation, unemployment and uncertainty, though with some undeniably exciting and rewarding moments.

The call for a general strike was taken up in Moscow. The Soviet in Moscow was a coalition of all socialist parties, but effective control was exercised by the all-Bolshevik party committee of the town. Since October the parties and the factory workers had been urging each other on to more zealous feats of revolution. In December the arrest of the Petersburg Soviet coincided with a feeling prevalent among soviet leaders in Moscow that an outlet must be found for so much pent-up popular indignation, regardless of how ill-prepared the workers might be. Their arms were pitifully inadequate and their plans non-existent. Even their conviction that all Russia would rise at their signal and overthrow the criminal regime, was undermined by a haunting fear that they were the victims of their own deception. Yet the party committee and the leaders of the Soviet had no choice but to go along with the mood which they themselves had created.[11]

The action was begun on 20 December by strikes spreading throughout the city's industrial districts. Simultaneously, armed workers commenced guerrilla operations, to seize weapons from the city police. The authorities reacted by declaring a state of emergency and calling for fresh troops, in spite of the fact that Moscow was well garrisoned with reliable soldiers, whose loyalty or obedience easily outweighed the unrest in some barracks. The intention of the governor-general of Moscow, Admiral Dubasov, was to deal quickly and effectively with this new outbreak of sedition. Police and troops together raided revolutionary meetings. Soviet leaders were arrested, and on 21 December armed strikers, gathered in a church building, were shelled by artillery which they answered with small-arms fire. Exchange of fire now began to take place in the open, on the main streets of the city, as bands of armed strikers encountered troops or police. Barricades were thrown across the main thoroughfares, though their value was symbolic rather than practical in view of the small forces available to the insurrectionaries.

The party men still at large in Moscow became increasingly aware that the uprising was a failure from the outset. They lacked means for coordinating the inadequate resources and they were forced to recognise the gross discrepancy between their forces and those of the state. After a week of sporadic and indecisive fighting the spirit went out of the insurgents, the Soviet agreed to call a halt. The last battle took place in the militant working-class district of Presnya, where the insurgents were subjected to brutally heavy shelling. By 30 December the military authorities had complete control once more and were able to carry out their punitive measures against suspects without hindrance.

The policy of armed uprising, so loudly and energetically proclaimed by all socialist parties, had been put into practice. Lenin's enthusiastic studies of street fighting, bomb-making and civil war, had at least been echoed by the Moscow workers, though he had not been there to witness the event. Witte's resolute Minister of the Interior, P. N. Durnovo,* continued this policy of firm action against all acts of rebellion. Summary executions were numerous; rebellious troops tired of waiting to be repatriated from the Far East were either hastily transported or in serious cases ruthlessly suppressed. Where at the beginning of the year the brutality of 'Bloody Sunday' had aroused anger and truculence in the population, now at the year's exhausted end it produced resignation and apathy. Known and suspected agitators and underground activists were deported in droves in order to liquidate the revolutionary organisations. Witte was aiming at civil peace by means of the outright elimination of the revolutionary sector.

* Appointed a week after the October Manifesto.

In April 1906, well after the government had recovered complete control of the situation in Russia and the tide of revolution had ebbed, the two Social Democratic factions convened in Stockholm a new congress, designated by the Bolsheviks as the 'Fourth', and by the Mensheviks as the 'Unification'. Its chief purpose was to unite all forces for the final onslaught against the Tsarist regime.

It was Lenin's declared belief that a new rising must come soon and that the party must be ready to act decisively. The government's policy of severe repression against the revolutionary movement made it all the more urgent in Lenin's eyes that party militancy should be heightened and transmitted to the widest sectors of the population. The question of whether or not to participate in elections to the Duma was dismissed by Lenin as secondary, a mere diversion. He even played down the importance of reorganising the party in favour of top priority for armed uprising. The agrarian platform, which he put forward at the Fourth Congress, and which exhorted the peasants to seize the land, he justified by claiming that in carrying it out the peasants would produce a major uprising in the process. And he added that it was up to the party to see that the workers were ready to support such a conflict with armed force.[12]

Lenin's attitude to the question of unification with the Mensheviks was summed up in his comment to Lunacharsky immediately before the congress opened: 'We won't permit the idea of unity to tie a noose round our necks, and we shall under no circumstances permit the Mensheviks to lead us on a rope.'[13]

Although the Mensheviks composed sixty per cent of the delegates to the congress, Lenin succeeded, by sheer force of argument and conviction, in carrying a number of debates in his own favour. For example, the majority now recognised that his formula for membership of the party, which had been rejected at the Second Congress, provided a better guarantee that initiative would be kept by the professional underground of the party, and it was accordingly accepted. This was an occasion when the

Narodnaya Volya tradition, explicit in Bolshevism, was revealed as a forgotten inheritance in Menshevism as well. The Mensheviks were, however, divided over this fundamental issue and their majority's line at the congress would not long survive.

On a more vital issue, the party's policy towards the peasants, Lenin advocated what he called 'nationalisation' of the land. What he had in mind was the peasants' seizure of the land as an integral and indispensable accompaniment to the workers' armed uprising. This view of revolution amounted to no less than the total disruption of state and social relationships. The Mensheviks succeeded in defeating Lenin's 'nationalisation' proposal and put forward instead the idea of 'municipalisation' of the land. Their ideas on this explosive subject were more constructive and derived from their recognition of the zemstvo's strength.

The unity achieved in Stockholm was no more than nominal. The debates revealed such fundamental differences of approach to cardinal issues that Lenin's intention to maintain his private apparatus, through which to exercise his ideas, seems in retrospect almost common sense. One such difference was over methods of financing the party's activities. The decline of the revolution which accompanied the government's repressive policy, had led to a sharp decline in the lavish donations from rich sympathisers on which the party had hitherto largely depended. It was now evident to these donors that the large and successful liberal parties were the better investment.

In the chaotic and lawless conditions of 1905 Lenin's fiery exhortations to his followers in Russia, to do anything to promote an armed uprising, had sometimes been understood as an incitement to crime. There were incidents of daylight robbery carried out in the name of the revolution. At Stockholm Lenin accepted the shocked view of the majority that the party must stop these seizures of money by individuals or groups, operating under the name of the party. But Lenin's own draft resolution on this question read: 'We should permit armed attacks for the purpose of seizing financial resources from the enemy, i.e. the autocratic government, and for the purpose of armed uprising. . . . These armed attacks by partisans should be carried out under the Party's supervision . . . .'[14] It was rather to Lenin's policy that the Bolsheviks adhered after the 'Unification' Congress of April 1906. Indeed, since the Mensheviks continued to be the party majority, Lenin leaned the more upon 'expropriations' to support his factional machine.

The most notorious 'expropriation' was carried out in Tiflis in June 1907, when a Bolshevik armed 'combat unit', under the local direction of Joseph Dzhugashvili (better known as Stalin), stole over 300,000 roubles.[15] The organisation which executed these operations was under the direct supervision of Lenin himself.* It was the imaginative Leonid Krasin who planned and furnished most of the Bolsheviks' major exploits of this nature, and who was also responsible even for forging banknotes. The Mensheviks were incensed by all these scandalous dealings, particularly since that year, at the Fifth Congress, the Bolsheviks had roundly condemned such actions. Lenin himself may have held other views.†

The issue of expropriations at the Fourth Congress concerned more than mere method for it arose against a background of wide political vistas. The revolutionary organisations in Russia may have been crushed by severe government measures, but on the other hand the country was alive with political activity. Elections to the forthcoming Duma were nearly over by the time of the Fourth Congress, and it was already clear that the Kadet party had won a major victory. The policy of boycotting the elections, which nearly all socialists had advocated (though not all had practised), was now a patent error, for the Social Democrats realised they had thus placed themselves outside the main arena. The openly criminal operations of Bolshevik armed bands served as a brutal

* One of Lenin's agents, Dr Jacob Zhitomirsky, appointed to handle the stolen money once it had been brought out of Russia, turned out to be a police spy.

† *Pyatyi (Londonskii) Syezd*, p. 583, shows Lenin as *against* this resolution. But Trotsky, *My Life*, p. 218, recalls that Lenin, who was chairman of the session, refrained from voting and merely 'chuckled, with a somewhat cryptic expression' when the delegates asked him to comment.

confirmation of this fact, and one to which the Mensheviks reacted sharply.

The Menshevik majority at the congress resolved that the Party should put up candidates wherever the elections had still to be fought. They would nonetheless always remain in two minds about 'parliamentarism' versus 'revolutionism', and would indeed attempt to preserve this duality in their thinking.[16] Subsequently, faced with Lenin's renewed recourse to illegality on the one hand, and the liberals' success on the other, the Mensheviks opted for 'revolutionary parliamentarism', that is, they would exploit the opportunities offered by the Duma for propaganda.

Lenin supported this resolution at the congress, although his own proposal made it plain that he regarded the Duma as a crude fraud and the elections as a cheap comedy. Bolshevik resolutions were in fact rather uncertain on this issue, taking an extremely negative line towards participation in the present elections, yet leaving open the question of future elections. Lenin's scepticism towards the Duma, shared by the Mensheviks and all other socialists, was well justified by subsequent events.

6

The Years of Reform

Witte had convinced the Tsar that civil peace could not be restored as a result of reforms alone, and that only the forced suppression of agitation would give both government and public the chance of properly evaluating the changes about to be introduced. Fear was widespread that further repression would only generate greater unrest, and even members of the government anticipated trouble when the Soviet was arrested *en masse*. The lack of response in the capital reinforced the government's conviction that its tough policy was the correct one.

While his Minister of the Interior, Durnovo, was busy stamping out local fires, Witte proceeded to implement the promises of Nicolas's October Manifesto. Government measures were influenced by the Tsar's ambivalence, on the one hand to make concessions, but on the other to retain complete control. Thus Witte issued a series of decrees which both confirmed the Tsar's promises and yet in some way restricted them.

The franchise, which had been promised as broad, turned out to be based on a system of indirect voting, with large landowners in a class apart; property qualifications were set for townsmen, thus restricting the participation of factory workers and city professionals. The Duma was clearly intended to have a class bias.

Freedom of the press was granted as promised, but with the rider that action would be taken against matter considered illegal, spreading false information about state officials, or for favourable comment on criminal acts. The mention of these legitimate limitations, which in normal circumstances any legal newspaper would impose upon itself, was meant to spell out to the liberals, who largely controlled the legal press, that their honeymoon with the revolutionaries must end.

The right of assembly and association was decreed in March 1906, with the 'assurance' that the police would see that meetings were orderly. This seemingly sensible precaution against the precipitation of new conflicts was also a weapon in the hands of the mostly anti-liberal administration, and it was used to great effect in disorganising liberal forces.

The publication of these and other decrees was received with much ill-feeling and suspicion. The public wondered what point there would be in having a Duma, if important legislation was going to be enacted in a flood of decrees on the eve of its opening ? Why was the government acting with such unseemly haste ? The most alarming sign of the government's intentions came on 7 May 1906, three days before the Duma was to be opened.[1] The government published what it called the Fundamental Laws as revised by Witte's cabinet, using this title as a euphemism for 'constitution' (a word which was anathema to Nicolas). Yet in the previous October Nicolas had proclaimed as an immutable principle that no law should come into effect without the approval of the State Duma. The publication of legislation, in the form of state decrees, on the very eve of the Duma's opening, was taken as a direct contradiction of the spirit of the October Manifesto, and as an assault on public initiative.

In fact there had been a good deal of debate among ministers and high officials as to the advisability of publishing the new Fundamental Laws before the Duma met. They had continually to reassure themselves that the electoral law would bring in a compliant assembly with a preponderance of loyal peasants' deputies. By pushing through certain legislation by decree, Witte hoped to load a mass of lesser projects on to the assembly in order to occupy it and keep it off dangerous issues.

Similarly, by borrowing the massive, and unprecedented, sum of 800 million gold roubles from foreign sources with which to finance his programme, he demonstrated that he was determined to be independent of any sanctions the Duma might seek to apply.

With the country now pacified and the government financially secure, Witte looked forward to easy manipulation of the Duma, and to this end he sought to remould the image of the government by getting rid of the repressive Durnovo. He chose to effect this move by threatening his own resignation. Unfortunately for him, the Tsar's attitude was that there was no longer any need for either Durnovo or Witte, and in one decree issued on 7 May they were both relieved of their posts—an act which must have gratified the Tsar as much as it mortified Witte. The tension created by the publication of the Fundamental Laws was increased by Witte's resignation, for, however much he was publicly distrusted, his presence in the government was seen as a counter-balance to the repressive habits of the old regime.

Feeling that enough ground had been given and that it was time for a period of conservation, Nicolas appointed a cabinet in which only one man was a recognised progressive, while all the rest were either entrenched conservatives or outright reactionaries. They were led by a cynical old bureaucrat, Goremykin, who would live to govern in still more critical times. The Tsar's choice of cabinet had also been affected by the results of the elections to the First Duma. For, although a large number of peasants' deputies had indeed been elected, it was emerging that, far from being the docile herd of patriots who would follow the directions of reactionary priests-turned-politicians, these peasants were identifying with the Kadets. The Duma was not going to be so easily manipulated after all.

The two trends of the Kadet party had revealed themselves during the election campaign. Among the peasants they had campaigned on the platform of free distribution of the land. To the educated public, however, they presented themselves as a reasonable and mature party that had learned its lesson. Here, they spoke of redistribution of the land, but with compensation. They dropped the demand for a constituent assembly and for a democratic republic. Now they stood for a parliamentary regime under a constitutional monarch, and on this. platform they achieved a large majority in the elections to the First Duma.[2]

The new legislature consisted of two chambers. The lower house was the State Duma, with 524 deputies, elected by indirect and complicated suffrage, which the government hoped would ensure a large number of carefully vetted peasants, wealthy land-owners and businessmen. The upper house was the State Council, remodelled so that now half its members were elected by the zemstvos, gentry assemblies, clergy, commercial and industrial institutions, the Academy of Sciences and the universities, and by the Finnish parliament; while the other half were appointed by the crown as before. It contained nearly 200 seats. To become law, legislation had to pass through both houses and then be approved by the sovereign.

The Tsar's choice of Council members was not invariably conservative or reactionary. Among the crown appointees as well as the elected members there were a number of Kadets and progressives. But the composition of the Council was designed to keep the Duma at a distance from the supreme power: as long as there was conflict between the two houses the Tsar need not be involved. In spite of its progressive members, the prevalent feeling in the Council was one of reluctance to contemplate the implications of the Tsar's Manifesto. Many, especially those appointed by the crown, were afraid to join the reformers whole-heartedly because they sensed the Tsar's disapproval. The Council thus came to be a shield between the Duma and the Monarch.

The Kadets owed their success in the elections to superior electoral methods. Their party attracted the largest number of party-minded men in political life, and they were experienced in running large-scale operations under the hostile gaze of the administration. They were the professionals, while the Octobrists shared with the socialists a lack of this political know-how. The Socialist Revolutionaries had boycotted the elections and the peasant votes they might have won went to the Kadets.

Lenin was hesitant at first about what course to take over the elections. But the Bolsheviks as a group felt that to take part in the elections would only lead the workers to believe that the Social Democratic programme could be achieved by peaceful, non-revolutionary, parliamentary means. The Duma would in any case be merely a tool of the government, and so it was the duty of Social Democrats to remain outside it, agitating the masses on any issue which arose between the government and the Duma, and exposing both in the worst possible light.

Like Lenin, the Mensheviks also hesitated at first. A major drawback for them, as well as for the Bolsheviks, was the fear of police interference, both in the elections and in the affairs of a Duma delegation. At the Fourth (Unification) Congress, however, they opted for an eleventh-hour attempt to capture seats, where elections were still to be fought. The Mensheviks in the Caucasus had already decided to take part, having seen in the Duma a platform for their national demands. They achieved twice as many votes as all the other parties in the Caucasus put together.

After the elections the Social Democrats either openly or implicitly admitted the mistake of their boycott. The workers had voted for the next best thing to a socialist candidate, a Kadet, or for the left-wing Kadet splinter group, called the Labourists (*Trudoviki*). This latter group consisted mainly of peasants and populist intellectuals, with some Socialist Revolutionaries who had ignored their party's directive. The leader of this group in the Fourth Duma was Alexander Kerensky.

There were twenty-six parties and sixteen national groups in the First Duma, which opened on 10 May. The alignment was simple: out of the 524 deputies 200 were peasants who voted either with the Kadets or with the Labour group. The Kadets had 180 seats, plus the usual support of 100 Labour votes and the national groups. The Social Democrats had only eighteen seats. To the right of the Kadets sat thirty to forty moderates, mainly

Octobrists, constituting the right wing of the Duma. It was thus an extremely leftward inclined assembly. Restraint could only come from the very small Octobrist group, and many of them were indistinguishable from the right wing of the Kadets.[3]

All Witte's legislation, which he had planned to put before the Duma, had been left in the drafting stage after his downfall. Thus when the Duma opened and the deputies waited eagerly to debate great national issues of economic and social consequence, they found instead that the government had nothing to offer, except two farcically petty matters, which drew an angry outburst of passion that might otherwise have been channelled into useful debate. In an address to the Tsar, the Duma virulently condemned the government, demanding universal suffrage and the direct vote, abolition of the upper house, a cabinet responsible to the Duma, a general political amnesty, and expropriation of the large estates and crown lands, as a prerequisite of land reform.

The reply came not from the Monarch but from the cabinet in its own name. Rejection of the Duma's demands was a foregone conclusion, but the imperious tone of the reply came as a shock and a goad. The Duma launched into debates on such explosive issues as police repression, pogroms, amnesty, land reforms, national discrimination and the independence of Poland. Already in the cabinet and court circles there were many who wanted the Duma to be dissolved immediately and a new one to be elected on a revised electoral law, designed to reduce the left wing. Yet the government was largely inert, except for the new Minister of the Interior, Peter Stolypin. Stolypin was appointed as a strong and experienced administrator who, though a conservative, was not a policeman like his predecessor. He opened talks with leaders of the Kadets and the Octobrists on the question of their participation in the cabinet. They failed because neither the moderates nor the Kadets could overlook Stolypin's known predilection for administrative methods. A proposal by Shipov that a new cabinet should be formed by the Kadets, the majority party in the Duma, was also entertained by Stolypin, though not seriously. The government had made up its mind to disperse the Duma and introduce a new electoral law.

During the two months of its existence the First Duma did little more than rage against the government. As the left wing had intended, the Duma proved to be a valuable sounding board, from which the revolutionary slogans of 1905 could echo throughout the country. The government had sufficient grounds to justify its dispersal of the turbulent Duma, but a particular coincidence of events hastened its action. Stolypin, having done his duty by talking to the Duma leaders, failed to find any common ground with them. Then there occurred a series of particularly sensational terrorist attacks. Simultaneously in the Duma the question was raised of appealing to the country against the government's report on the agrarian question.

For two months the government had been pointing out to Nicolas that the inflammatory speeches being made in the Duma, without restraint from any moderating parties, were rekindling the embers of 1905. Yet the military commandant of the capital reported that no unrest was expected to follow the decree dispersing the Duma, and he was proved right. In these propitious circumstances Nicolas signed the dissolution decree. Goremykin was dismissed in favour of Stolypin.

The dissolution of the First Duma in July 1906 marked a turn in progressive politics. The right wing of the Kadets went into the Octobrist party, where they felt free at last from the hazards of left-wing alliances. For the Octobrists and the progressives in general the dissolution meant the end of the hope that a government might be formed to unite state and society, to realise the promise of 1905 and work for the peaceful transformation of the regime.[4]

The majority of Kadets, however, took up the dissolution as a challenge. They gathered together in the Finnish port of Vyborg, seventy-five miles away, and issued a manifesto calling on the people not to pay their taxes and not to send their sons at the next call-up. It was a call to civil disobedience, and its main purpose was to arouse as wide a protest as possible to the government's arbitrary treatment of the people's elected representatives. But like the dissolution of the Duma itself, the appeal evoked no response from the masses.

The failure of the Vyborg appeal greatly encouraged the reactionaries at court, who could now urge the government not to be afraid of hindering further changes.

Stolypin, while he had no intention of sharing power with the liberal opposition, was sufficiently realistic to recognise that the government's measures must prove to the people that its welfare and future were the government's chief concern. Equally they must prove to the liberal opposition that it need no longer suspect the government of bad faith. Stolypin's policy was to improve the lot of the people while at the same time strengthening the power and prestige of the regime.

The summer of 1906, when the Duma was in recess and Stolypin was busy preparing his programme of reforms, was also a period of intense revived terrorism. The object of the terror was multiple: to recapture public attention while the liberals were deprived of their Duma platform; further to antagonise relations between the government and the opposition and thus compromise the new Duma in advance; and to disrupt the government's intention to introduce important new and possibly popular reforms. But the terror did not deflect Stolypin, even though his own house was destroyed and his two small children injured—an event which moved the Tsar sufficiently to establish military courts martial to deal with the terrorists. Such a measure was unwelcome to Stolypin, as he was determined to achieve the pacification of the country through quasi-constitutional means, and not by punitive measures which had a habit of rebounding. The Tsar's declaration of a state of emergency on 1 September, after the attempt on Stolypin, and the counter-terror activities of the various Black Hundred organisations, some of which were patronised at court, frustrated Stolypin's objects. But in these circumstances he felt justified in introducing new laws under Article 87 of the Fundamental Laws, which permitted legislation under extraordinary circumstances during a recess of the Duma.

Land reform was the most crying need. Stolypin's first act was to increase the amount of land available for purchase by the peasants, by transferring all state and crown land to the Peasants' Bank. The economic effect of this measure was not great, but Stolypin was after a psychological effect, as well as an economic and social one. Related to this issue was the question of the peasants' legal ties with the commune, which also impinged on the whole question of agrarian efficiency and peasant discontent. By a decree of 22 November 1906 peasants were allowed to leave the commune without first asking its permission, and were also allowed to own in perpetuity the land they tilled for the commune.

Between 1906 and 1910, through the loophole of Article 87, Stolypin managed to put through a series of agrarian measures which, according to his own formula, were intended to create a class of strong and independent farmers. Every peasant house-holder, in those communes which redivided their land (i.e. three-quarters of all communes), was permitted to take private possession of the land he farmed. All communal land was to be distributed to the new individual farmers as their own property. Joint family ownership was abolished and the family head was recognised as the owner.

Now peasants were not only free to move about the country like other classes of the population, but they were also liberated from the supervision of the Land Captains, who had had the authority to fine them or send them to prison. Stolypin was aiming at the spiritual as well as the economic regeneration of the peasants.

Reforms were introduced to consolidate scattered strips, and where necessary to redistribute them. To facilitate this, local commissions were set up. The process of land acquisition by the peasantry which had been going on since 1861 was greatly accelerated, so that by 1916 the peasants were by far the largest landowning class.

Like Witte before him, Stolypin had to contend with a substantial block of opposition, both within the government and from the court, which constantly asked whether the government was not trying to do too much too soon. Particularly unpopular with his right-wing colleagues was his proposed legislation to permit freedom of religious belief. This had already been raised in 1903 but not implemented. Now Stolypin proposed to permit any group of at least twenty people sharing the same religious belief to be recognised as a religious community, provided their tenets of faith did not call for immoral acts, but no matter how opposed they were to the Orthodox faith. This was an extreme reform, in view of the government's history of severe repression of all forms of religious 'deviation'. The cabinet opposition to this measure succeeded in getting Stolypin to abandon the idea, for the question of religious tolerance, it was feared, touched on the loyalty of whole nations living within the empire.

Freedom of religion also involved the question of civil rights for certain alien groups still almost totally unfranchised. The Jews were the most significant of these groups, since they figured prominently in the professions and public life. Stolypin's critics were mortified by his proposal, not only to allow religious freedom to such as the Jews, but also to let out of the Pale of Settlement a wider range of Jewish categories. They protested that the Jews had played a large part in 1905, and now the government was proposing to reward them for it. Yet, surprisingly, in the end the cabinet approved Stolypin's project, and it was left to the Tsar to reject it.

The Social Democrats and the Socialist Revolutionaries both took an active part in the election to the Second Duma. The extreme right-wing parties and the Orthodox clergy, who had ignored the First Duma, were encouraged and often subsidised, by private and government-sponsored groups, to put up candidates. The Ministry of the Interior secretly directed the local police to inhibit the campaigning of any party that seemed hostile to the government. In practice this meant harassing the Kadets. The Kadets were badly hit by the fact that the 200 deputies of the First Duma who had supported the Vyborg Manifesto had been deprived of the right to re-enter the Duma, as well as being disfranchised, imprisoned for three months, and humiliated by the fact that the public had not uttered a sound in response to their Vyborg appeal. The Kadets were more affected than any other party by the prohibition on public employees from taking part in the election, thus eliminating the zemstvo professionals. The police forcibly disorganised Kadet meetings, thugs were employed to intimidate and threaten candidates; two of the Kadets' leading figures, both Jews, one of them their most eloquent spokesman on the land question, were murdered.[5]

The attention lavished by the administration on the Kadet campaign achieved its effect, but at the cost of making the Duma altogether unworkable. The Kadets were indeed reduced, from 180 to 92. But the Social Democrats now numbered sixty-five, of whom eighteen were Bolsheviks; the Socialist Revolutionaries got forty-eight seats; the Labour group remained around 100. The support that the Kadets had enjoyed from the 200 peasants in the First Duma was seriously reduced by the incursion of the clergy and right-wing groups. The Octobrists remained around thirty. Twenty-two seats were held by the extreme right wing, a genuine lunatic fringe. National and regional groups, Poles, Cossacks, Muslims, accounted for 160 votes, but had no opportunity to profit from their strength in this, the most unconstructive, Duma. Finally the government could count on the votes of at least ninety deputies.[6]

If the First Duma had been truculent, the Second was openly revolutionary. It lasted from 5 March to 16 June. Sessions were conducted in uproar, as the extreme left and right hurled abuse at each other and as both abused the Kadets sitting in between. The Kadets now realised that the very foundation of the Duma was at stake. But they did nothing to dissociate themselves from the demarcation of the revolutionary parties. They were plainly afraid to jeopardise their popularity, but they thus left themselves open to right-wing attack. The Second Duma was completely sterile, since all the political elements in it cancelled each other out.

Stolypin had prepared a vast programme of legislation with

which he confronted this new and totally unsuitable assembly. Stolypin's programme included his measures for land reform, freedom of religion, inviolability of the person, civic equality, workers' national insurance, income tax reform, reform of the zemstvos, introduction of zemstvos in the Baltic and western provinces; compulsory primary education, reform of secondary and high schools; police reform.

In an address to the Duma Stolypin proclaimed that the basis of all the government's bills was the general principle that Russia must become a legal state, that written law must define the duties and protect the rights of individual Russian subjects, to ensure that these rights and duties were not dependent on the interpretation or authority of individuals. He thus proclaimed the constitutional state, the very pivot of liberal ethics. Indeed, Stolypin was making an attempt to raise the hopes of the liberals, in order precisely to procure their support for his projects.

The assembly listened to Stolypin's address with rapt attention, and later Milyukov remarked that no European would have understood how after such a declaration a vote of no confidence could take place. But a violent attack was launched against the government's programme by the Georgian Social Democrat, Tseretelli, which amounted to a full cry for revolution. Others joined him from the left and centre, seizing the opportunity to keep up pressure on the government and rekindle revolutionary ardour.

For Stolypin it was a shock. He had thought his speech would find an echo. Instead he discovered, what he must have suspected, that the left was not interested in the legislative function of the Duma but only in its value as a platform for revolutionary propaganda. He told a silent assembly that the government would welcome exposure of any irregularity, that it was seeking a common language with the Duma; but it would not tolerate threats of revolution.

Stolypin did not want to let the Kadets hang themselves. He wanted his reforms to have the constitutional hallmark which the Duma could give them, and for the time being he still thought this possible, without turning the Duma into a rubber stamp.

The right-wing parties were busy from the moment the Second Duma opened campaigning for its closure and for amendment of the electoral laws. The Kadets, who realised that they were almost the only party with a stake in the Duma, tried to secure their left flank by introducing a bill calling for the abolition of the courts martial which the Tsar had ordered to be set up *ad hoc* to deal with terrorists, and which Stolypin had regretted.

The Kadets' attempt to get the government to abolish the courts martial brought from Stolypin an even more open appeal to the centre. He told the Duma that whether the extraordinary measures would remain in force was a matter for it to decide. But, as a mark of their good faith, the Duma must condemn all the bloodshed and extremism which the courts martial were there to deal with. The government, he said, did not want to keep these measures in force, but wanted to return to peaceful and constructive work. Stolypin wanted to silence the right-wing critics of the Duma by making the Kadets show their 'constitutional' face. He requested Milyukov to condemn terrorism either through the Kadet party, or in his newspaper, even anonymously: 'Just condemn murder.' The reward would be a guarantee of peace for the Kadet party. Milyukov, thinking that an unhampered Kadet party would be the salvation of the Duma, agreed on condition that the party leaders approve. He spoke to Petrunkevich, who was horrified: 'You are ruining your own reputation and dragging the party with you . . . No, never! Better sacrifice the party itself than induce its moral decay.' Instead of writing the article against revolutionary murder, Milyukov turned his literary talent to condemning right-wing murders and terror.[7] He thus did nothing to strengthen Stolypin's hand against the right. Stolypin's decision to disperse the unworkable assembly was now merely a matter of time and opportunity.

The excuse to dissolve the Duma came when the police presented faked evidence that the Social Democrat deputies, both Bolsheviks and Mensheviks, had contact with revolutionary cells in the armed forces, and that a conspiracy to assassinate the Tsar and ferment mutiny had been uncovered. Stolypin demanded the exclusion of the Social Democrat deputies. The Duma appointed a committee to discuss Stolypin's demand, but by the next day had not come to a decision. Stolypin had already decided that, if by that day the Duma had not ejected its Social Democrat deputies, he would issue the Imperial decree of dissolution, and this he did.

The same day, 16 June, Stolypin promulgated a new electoral law, which had been in preparation since before the Second Duma met. It simply increased the number of deputies who could be elected by landowners, and reduced the number for whom workers and peasants could vote. This act was a flagrant violation of the constitution and amounted to a *coup d'état*. But by this time it was doubtful whether the shock that greeted this imperious act was genuine. The public was by now accustomed to the government's capricious approach to politics, though there is also little doubt that capriciousness was a characteristic common to both sides and all factions in Russian political life.

Stolypin's new electoral law completely changed the composition of the Duma. From 521 in the Second, the total number of deputies was reduced to 442 in the Third. The Octobrists, who were the only party prepared to collaborate with the government, in order to preserve the Duma in being, now held 150 seats, an increase over their numbers in the Second Duma of more than 100. On the extreme right wing were grouped about 150 members, including the anti-government right wing which was opposed to the government's 'surrender to liberal doctrine'. From these two sectors Stolypin gradually built up his own support to about eighty. The Kadets were reduced to fifty-three seats, with support from twenty-eight left-Kadet deputies, reorganised as Progressists. The new law had hit hardest at the extreme left. In the Second Duma the Social Democrats, Socialist Revolutionaries, Labourists and Populists had together amounted to 214; in the Third Duma the figure was below thirty. Equally the national and regional groups were severely curtailed by the new law. This 'rubber stamp' parliament of Stolypin's was intended to embody *Russian* ideals, and its relations with the government were to be calm and harmonious. On these conditions the government was prepared to minister to society the medicine prescribed by the spokesmen of the left and centre.

The Third Duma reflected the general mood of the country. If reforms could be instituted without recourse to violence and social disruption, the overwhelming mass of the population was doubtlessly satisfied that this should be so. To the public Stolypin's reforms seemed patently beneficial, notably his land reform, which was an open invitation to initiative and vigour. Society could not but be heartened by his decision to 'bank on the strong, individual proprietors, and not on the weak and drunken'.

Stolypin was in fact banking on more than this, for his programme was permeated with a spirit of Great Russian nationalism, even chauvinism, by which he intended to engender a pact with the 'real' Russian people. By curbing the non-Russian nationalities of the empire, while simultaneously enacting liberal reforms for the Russian peasantry, Stolypin could not fail to create an impression of the government's good intentions for the Russian people, as a distinct group. The progressives might be appalled by this blatantly reactionary approach and see in it an omen of future cataclysms, but the average Russian citizen preferred to see it as a means of strengthening the best, the fundamental elements of the empire, namely, the Russian.

But Stolypin's chief enemies were not on the left. It was the right wing who opposed his programme of breaking up the traditional institutions of Russian society—the peasant commune and the established system of classes. Moreover, Stolypin's powers seemed like an affront to the paternalistic monarchy, which they cherished. A serious setback in his relations with the Tsar came in a paradoxical way. In 1910 he introduced a bill for establishing zemstvos in six western provinces, but ensuring the supremacy of Russian over Polish elements. (Jews were excluded altogether.) The Duma succeeded in achieving some mitigating amendments, but when the upper house discussed it, in February 1911, eight months after its first appearance, they rejected it for the reason that it curtailed the privileges of the Polish nobility, who were entitled to be treated as such. The majority included an extreme right-wing group who were known to be favoured by the Tsar.

Stolypin was now politically isolated, for the Duma, the State Council majority, and a court party, had all come out against him. Five years of power and success had made him less tolerant of opposition than before. Faced with defeat, he reacted angrily and tendered his resignation. When Nicolas asked him to reconsider, he made terms: suspension of both houses for three days, introduction of his bill under Article 87 and suspension of his most hostile opponents. The Tsar agreed but Stolypin's star had faded. Already he had incurred the personal animosity of the Empress for having made an unfavourable report on the activities of Rasputin, who by 1911 had become a notorious influence in the royal family life.

In September 1911, Stolypin, aged only forty-nine, but ill and isolated, met an untimely death. The occasion was the royal visit to Kiev for the unveiling of a memorial to Alexander II, to be followed by a gala performance at the Kiev opera. Special security measures had been taken, the city swarmed with police and security agents. An ex-police informer, Dmitri Bogrov, was planted in the theatre to keep watch for alleged assassins. Bogrov, however, intent on purging himself of guilt as a revolutionary, turned assassin himself. At point-blank range he shot Stolypin, who died a few days later. Bogrov was hanged before a proper investigation could be conducted. The security authorities in Kiev and St Petersburg were widely suspected of having executed a plan originated by right-wing circles, but nothing was ever established.[8]

While the question of Stolypin's death remains an open one, the success of his policies is less open to doubt. In the period 1909–14 Russia's economic output was greatly stimulated. The highest point in her economy was reached between the summer of 1912 and summer of 1914. The standard of living went up to twice that of 1894. Money was more plentiful, savings went up seven-fold. Local crafts and services were rejuvenated as a result of the new flow of money in the villages. The health of the Russian economy was demonstrated by the fact that, although no new taxes were introduced after 1894, and no increases were made in existing taxation, by 1914 the gold reserve of the state bank grew from 648,000,000 gold roubles to 1,604,000,000. It was a demonstration of Russia's economic vitality that, although between 1912 and 1914 a succession of economic strikes took place, yet with the declaration of war the workers permitted no grievance against the regime to blur their patriotic enthusiasm.

Amid the unprecedented prosperity, there reigned an un-precedented mood of political indifference, which alarmed all sectors of political opinion. Right and left feared that this 'drifting' would lead to some sort of bourgeois society in Russia. The relative prosperity of the urban workers, and the property which gave the peasants their stake in a stable Russia were seen by the socialists as obstacles to the development of class antagonism and militancy; the right saw in these developments the decay of the class system and traditional relationships in the country-side, which were the guarantee of national stability. Political indifference also appalled the liberals and moderates, who felt robbed of their purpose and of their political future: if the government could succeed in bringing about the better part of the liberal programme without their help, then not only was their basis of opposition undermined, but their claim to power also.

Public apathy to economic and social issues made other flaws in the system assume greater proportions. Public attention was increasingly drawn to the court itself.

The object of this attention was the fatal relationship of the Empress with the illiterate and debauched peasant, the 'man of God', Rasputin. In 1904 the Empress had at last given birth to a son, a Tsarevich. But the parents' joy was dashed by the discovery that the child, Alexei, suffered from haemophilia, transmitted through his mother's family. Already the Empress had withdrawn from her Russian environment, preferring the simple solitude of her own family to the clamour of high society. Her son's tragedy threw her more ardently into seeking spiritual help and comfort, especially in the absence of a known cure for the disease. The court was increasingly frequented by purveyors of Orthodox spiritual solace and unorthodox medical aid.

Rasputin entered the Empress's life as early as 1905, when he was already becoming fashionable among high female society in the capital. He preached the doctrine of redemption through sin (equated for expediency with sex), and seemed bent on procuring as much redemption for his elegant disciples as his prodigious, indeed legendary, powers, would permit. Rasputin made himself indispensable to his Empress by his ability to stop the flow of blood by hypnosis whenever the young Alexei suffered a haemorrhage. He was the answer to her prayers, the very embodiment of crude, peasant, Holy Russia, possessed of the answers to life's unfathomable problems, answers which were themselves often unfathomable, but no less welcome for that.

As his influence with the Empress grew, so he became an object of exploitation by unscrupulous political and financial adventurers, with whom he was willing to trade upon his connections. Rasputin's 'private' life, which the royal couple persistently overlooked, offered itself to the opposition as the Tsar's Achilles' heel. When the opposition and even Stolypin, tried to intervene, the Empress forbade public discussion of the subject. In April 1912, Guchkov, the leader of the Octobrists, publicly denounced Rasputin in the Fourth Duma, and the Duma chairman, Rodzyanko, conveyed his own misgivings to the Tsar. The only result of their petition was to engender the Empress's lasting hatred of politicians and their Duma.

The lonely and hysterical Empress leaned increasingly on her miracle-worker, gradually coming to rely on his magic to solve even matters of state. For his part Rasputin continued to play the oracle, uttering in obscure pseudo-biblical jargon the words she most wanted to hear, and no doubt daily counting his blessings while they still lasted. As for the opposition, it had to await a more anxious national mood before the Rasputin lever could be manipulated.

7

The Party in Disarray

The prevalent mood in Russia after the dissolution of the Second Duma in June 1907, and indeed earlier, was that of a society surfeited with politics. Even for educated society, let alone the great mass of the peasantry and the workers, politics had been a diversion. The events of 1905 and the great stir caused by the creation of the State Duma had aroused universal interest and concern. But by 1907, the general feeling was that political agitation had ceased to be a force for liberation, and had become a threat to social and personal security. The years 1907–14 are sometimes designated the 'years of reaction'. This should be understood as the reaction of society, in the broadest sense. The state, on the other hand, was, as we have seen, energetically pursuing a programme of social and economic reform, the very antithesis of reaction.

The outlook of many Social Democrats also changed. There was a growing tendency to swim with the cultural current that was transforming the intellectual life of Europe. From militancy, the mood of the party changed to languor. A revolution of sorts had at last taken place in Russia, and the revolutionaries felt, and indeed were, bereft of purpose. There was nothing left for pro-fessional organisers to organise, nothing with which pro-fessional conspirators could conspire. Instead they were thrown back into the enervating vacuum of émigré politics, factional

sparring, ideological debate. Only Lenin continued his single-
minded crusade with undiminished zeal, but in this atmosphere
he was repeatedly frustrated by the consequences of his own
excess.

The Fifth Congress, held in London in April–May 1907, was
one of the most representative congresses ever held by the
RSDRP. It was attended by nearly 300 delegates. Everybody
associated with the leadership of the party since its beginnings
was there, plus a great many lesser, unknown figures, like Joseph
Stalin. Lenin controlled a variable majority with the support of
the Poles and Letts, while the Mensheviks could count on the
support of the Jewish *Bund* and thus maintain an almost equal
balance. An independent position was taken up by Trotsky, who
was emerging as a separate force within the Social Democratic
party.

In addition to being representative of some of the nationalities,
the congress was a fair reflection of the continuing dissension and
disunity in the party, which the Fourth (Unification) Congress of
April 1906 had done nothing to lessen. Throughout the proceedings the delegates heard 'Bolshevik', 'Menshevik', 'ours',
and 'yours'—the division was fixed hard, only slightly varied by
the special interests of the national groupings.

In spite of his slender majority, Lenin failed to gain outright
control of the new central committee elected by the congress. The
committee now reflected the factional proportions of the party,
with five Bolsheviks, four Mensheviks, and two each from the
Bund, the Poles, and the Letts. The functions of the new committee, were, however, now redefined to conform entirely to the
Leninist concept of the single centre, with control over the central
organ and its editors. It seemed that Lenin had at last succeeded
in bringing the party round to his point of view on organisation, yet no more than a week after the congress closed he found
himself isolated from his own faction on the major question of the
Duma.

The story of Social Democracy and the Duma had so far not

been a happy one. Both factions had been in two minds about taking part in elections to the First, and had thus let slip the chance to make a show of representing the working masses. The Mensheviks had changed their minds when they realised that Kadet militancy against the right wing was winning the workers away from Social Democracy. Lenin had also changed his mind; he now saw that the extremely militant peasant deputies had turned the Duma into a national platform for revolutionary propaganda. Lenin's change of position was, however, made painful for him by the fact that his followers were less nimble, and were reluctant to relinquish their 'Bolshevik' attitude towards the 'parliamentary comic opera'. They were proving to be more 'Leninist' than Lenin, and went on calling for boycott.

Between the election to the Second Duma in January–February 1907 and the Fifth Congress in May, Lenin succeeded in softening this attitude considerably, mainly by pointing out the enormous revolutionary potential of the peasant deputies, which no one had expected. But when, on returning from the Fifth Congress, the Social Democrats' Duma deputies were first framed by the government, then arrested and exiled, and the blame for the dissolution of the Second Duma was placed squarely on their shoulders, the Bolshevik boycotters reopened their campaign. At two successive conferences held in July and August 1907, in Finland, Lenin had to endure voting with the Mensheviks and the *Bundists* against his own faction. On the second occasion, indeed, he was the sole Bolshevik among the 'opportunists'.

Lenin was now in a precarious position and it wore his nerves. Militant Bolshevism had cut loose from its progenitor and had turned to the leadership of the Marxist mystic-philosopher, Bogdanov, until recently Lenin's chief executive. Any other Bolshevik in Lenin's position would automatically have found himself thrust into the enemy faction by scathing and destructive criticism. For Lenin this threat could not exist. However severe the disapproval of the Bolshevik majority, Lenin need never fear that he might overstep the factional borderline, for it was he who delineated it. His position was, however, a constant reminder to him that his followers were not yet disciples.

The ardour of the Bolshevik boycotters was eventually cooled by grim reality. Severe police repression and the workers' renewed concern for economic standards rather than political expression, decimated the ranks of the party during the Stolypin period. The Fifth Congress had exulted over a total membership of 150,000, including the national parties and the *Bund*. By 1910 the figure was estimated at 10,000, while the total number of Bolshevik committees in Russia amounted to no more than five or six.[1] Between 1907 and 1912 the Russian Social Democratic Party existed more in the minds of the factional leaders than anywhere else.

As for the eighteen beseiged Social Democrats in the Third Duma, they had to contend with hostile and carping criticism from the militant Bolsheviks. Lenin's demand for a revolutionary strategy within the Duma was constantly held up before their unwilling eyes. Their necessarily cautious behaviour in the Duma earned them contempt from their comrades outside. They soon learned that revolutionary tactics inside parliament were futile in the absence of any hope of response from outside. Only the most recalcitrant revolutionary could doubt, in the years of the Third Duma, that this lack was genuine. Regrettably for the Bolshevik deputies, their cautious tactics could be identified with the frank 'opportunism' of their Menshevik colleagues, who made no attempt to hide their support of the Kadets.

The Stolypin period was for the Social Democrats the time of their greatest estrangement from Russia and Russian affairs, of their minimum impact on the workers. As a result, the party itself became once again the object and main concern of its leaders. Every possible issue became the excuse for a new sub-division in one or another faction. Lenin's own apparatus, such as it was in those lean years, was divided at its head, the Bolshevik Centre, over the faction's Duma policy, and over Lenin's drive for a final and total break with the Mensheviks. In four years, from 1903 to 1907, Lenin had used the device of a party congress four times to establish his position and solidify his support. Now it would be ten years before the next party congress was convened to define the Bolshevik identity, and then, ironically, Lenin would be absent.

The unity of the party was threatened not only by Lenin's divisive and monopolistic attitudes. The Mensheviks were outraged by his continued use of the 'expropriations' as a means of financing his factional operations.[2] Apart from the 'expropriations', the Bolsheviks ran a succession of dubious financial operations, in secret from the Menshevik and other members of the Central Committee, which eventually became notorious. For instance, Lenin despatched two of his own agents to extort an inheritance from two sisters called Schmidt, whose father had left his estate to the entire party. Both agents married the girls to secure the funds, but the first one had to be threatened with his life before he could be made to part with his share, amounting to 100,000 roubles, or £10,000. The second, who became better known later as the Comintern agent, Victor Taratuta, succeeded in transferring into the Bolshevik coffers a sum of around £28,000. Again, the Bolsheviks diverted funds intended for the whole party from the estate of Morozov, the Moscow millionaire. As much as ideology, the continual jealous struggle for control of the party's funds, especially in view of the prodigious sums involved, made unity impossible.

Lenin's espousal of shady methods, and shadier operators to apply them, also alarmed some Bolsheviks. But his explanation was tough and realistic: 'This isn't a school for young ladies. . . . Sometimes a crook is useful to us just because he is a crook.' When Lenin proposed Taratuta as a Central Committee candidate he justified him as 'an intelligent crook'. Taratuta would stoop lower than anyone else in order to serve the Party's interests, and therefore he was of particular value in Lenin's eyes.[3] Lenin's negligence of party honour led many of his closest associates to desert him. His compromise over the Duma, his devious attitude towards the Mensheviks—working for a split but keeping up the pretence of unity—and his continued resort to criminal methods, all combined to brand him an opportunist in the eyes of some of his old comrades, not least those who like Bogdanov and Krasin had been his enthusiastic executives in precisely these operations: such firebrands would brook no compromise.

Life in exile, particularly the renewed, second spell, after the failure of 1905, was a moral and emotional ordeal. In a letter to Gorky, Lenin wrote in 1910 that exile was a hundred times harder than before 1905, and that exile and squabbles were inseparable.[4] It was harder to keep up the monolithic front of revolutionary zeal and camaraderie in the aftermath of 1905, not that the latter had ever been easy for the Russian Social Democrats. Indeed, it seemed to be in their very nature to find points of difference, rather than affinity. One looks in vain for any extended period during which the party was anything but a cacophony of dissonant voices. Only Stalin succeeded eventually in harmonising the chorus, but his methods can only be regarded as grotesque.

The fractiousness and jealous truculence of Russian Social Democrats on the eve of the war was cogently expressed by Rosa Luxemburg. Writing to Kautsky about a plan to call a conference of all the rival Russian groups, in an effort once and for all to settle their fight over the party's funds, she said that it was a foolish idea, for such a conference would only be attended by a 'handful of fighting cocks *living abroad* . . . and to expect anything of *these* cocks is pure delusion. They are already so . . . embittered, that a general confab will merely give them an opportunity to unburden themselves of their old, oldest and freshest insults. . . .'[5]

The issues between the factions, and between Lenin and his own Bolshevik dissidents, assumed as always their own labels, convenient as targets of abuse and factional crusades. Thus Bolsheviks who resisted Lenin's splitting tactics and worked for party unity were dubbed 'Conciliators', a word which was common party usage to describe the Kadets' and Octobrists' supposed relations with the government. On the other hand, the left-wing Bolsheviks, under Bogdanov's influence, who attacked the Social Democrat deputies in the Duma for their caution and campaigned to have them 'recalled', received the title of 'recallists' and their deviation 'Recallism'.

Some Mensheviks Lenin found guilty of a particularly heinous heresy: realising that the party apparatus was in ruins and under permanent threat from the police, these Mensheviks called on the party to concentrate its efforts on whatever legal activities could serve the workers' cause, such as trade unions, cooperatives, and supporting progressive legislation in the Duma. This approach was bad enough, and earned for them the Leninist curse of Reformism. But they went further and averred that these legal activities of the party should no longer be controlled by the underground centre, but should be left to develop organically in the prevailing social conditions.

To Lenin this was mutiny against central authority. To make his case stronger he, as always, overstated it and claimed that the movement was in favour of *liquidating* the party apparatus, though this was not intended. 'Liquidationism' was perhaps the most serious hindrance to unity, assuming that unity had any chance whatever, for it also split the Mensheviks. In 1909 Plekhanov rallied those Mensheviks who stood for 'the party', meaning the underground apparatus, and this group gained the title of 'partyists'.

Lenin's frustration in this period was compounded of more than mere difficulties over Menshevik claims to 'his' money, or a persistent cycle of dissidence among his supposed followers: he was being dragged out of his element by dramatic changes taking place in intellectual life and having their impact on Bolshevik intellectuals no less than any others. It was no coincidence that philosophical debate broke out among Bolshevik intellectuals at the same time as the Russian intelligentsia, coming to terms with the decline of revolution, were turning away from politics and becoming absorbed with metaphysics and morals. Lenin, who had been virtually isolated from his own faction from 1907 until 1909, was well aware that his troubles flowed from the very people, such as Bogdanov, who had joined him in 1904.

Like this philosopher-revolutionary, many of them were

primarily concerned with the cultural and moral aspects of revolution; the revolution was for the liberation and exaltation of Man, not for a redistribution of national wealth under the auspices of a proletarian dictatorship. It was Lenin's dynamism that had first attracted them to him. Bogdanov associated with the writer Maxim Gorky, the historian Pokrovsky, as well as Lunacharsky and others. They were, to Lenin, the reincarnation of the plague of the 1890s, the Economists, the Legal Marxists, the Revisionists. They were Russian intellectuals with a taste for violent revolution.* In 1908 they presumed to apply their intellectual detachment to a new appraisal of Marxism in philosophical terms. Lenin determined to make this the *casus belli* which would purge his faction once and for all of clever dissenters, who had tripped him up over his Duma policy, and were now inviting free discussion on a subject which for Lenin was holy writ. He had the still valuable support of the once unanswerable Plekhanov, whose orthodoxy was now a source of great comfort to Lenin.

In a long, discursive work, entitled *Materialism and Empiriocriticism, Critical Notes Concerning One Reactionary Philosophy*, and published in May 1909, Lenin aimed his first philosophical salvos against the 'revisionist' and 'reactionary' views being aired by Bogdanov. His terms were philosophical but his purpose was entirely political, namely, to recapture full authority in his 'own' faction, and to oust the presumptuous Bogdanov.

He castigated all the other Bolshevik deviations that were associated with Bogdanov, as well as laying on Bogdanov's shoulders the heresy of 'God-building', which did not properly belong to him.

'God-building', as propagated by Maxim Gorky, Lunacharsky and Bazarov, was the attempt by well-meaning materialists to counteract the metaphysical climate of the period by proclaiming socialism to be the only true religion of the people. God's attributes, they asserted, are no more than those of Man, made perfect. Therefore through socialism, which is the 'collectivity'

---

* In 1919 *The Times* described Lunacharsky as a 'Bolshevik crank' who 'dabbles in Bolshevism as he dabbles in art'.

of Man, mankind can and will create its own God, as the apotheosis of its highest goals. 'God-building' was related to the neo-Kantian revival that had an impact on intellectual life in Russia after 1905. It was particularly horrifying to Lenin in that it postulated a God, instead of being content with a Categorical Imperative. Writing to Maxim Gorky in November 1913 he expressed his view that all this 'intellectual necrophilia', this talking about gods and devils instead of attacking all religions, was a hundred times worse than saying nothing at all on the subject.

Lenin's hostility to the discussion of religious and metaphysical questions was intense. The mixture of physical disgust and sexual imagery is apparently unique in his available writings: '... any religious idea ... is the most dangerous abomination, the most prurient "contamination". The mob can more easily uncover a million sins, obscenities, assaults and *physical* contaminations, which are thus less dangerous, than the *subtle* ... idea of a god, decked out in elegant "theoretical" clothes. The Catholic priest who deflowers young girls (I happen to have been reading about one just now ...) is *far* less of a danger to "democracy" than a priest without a cassock, a priest without a crude religion, an intellectual, democratic priest preaching the building and creation of dear little gods.' He castigated Gorky for pandering to the narcissism of the dull-witted petty bourgeoisie. God-building was self-deception, for it was the philistines' substitute for 'acts', it was escape into fantasy of the 'disenchanted and tired', it was self-abasing. The scabby bourgeoisie was everywhere an abomination, but the 'democratic petty bourgeoisie, busy at intellectual necrophilia, is twice the abomination'.[6]

'Acts' constituted the basis of Lenin's philosophy; he could never reconcile himself to what he saw as Gorky's and the others' substitute for 'acts', their search for an ethic to fill the void following 1905. Lenin was still serious about the socialist revolution; indeed in 1910, the nadir of the revolutionary movement and its hopes, Akselrod could say of Lenin that he was the only man who gave his whole life to revolution, who lived for nothing else, and who even dreamed of revolution.[7]

Lenin's longing for revolution during the Stolypin era was in no way diminished by his recognition that the government was pursuing a resolute and well-conceived policy of social reform. Given twenty years of peace, at home and abroad, Stolypin was convinced that Russia would be transformed into a stable, responsible, property-owning society. Neither he nor the peace were to endure that long, but the changes which were achieved indicated that Stolypin's vision was less utopian and more practicable than the proposals and prognostications of most of his critics. One of the most astute of these was Lenin, who did not hide from the fact that the success of Stolypin's policy was a possibility. Lenin realised that the completion of the policy, 'before the proletarian revolution', would signify the '*final* consolidation of private ownership of *all* the land, both gentry and peasant'.[8]

But in the process of change produced by Stolypin's reforms he saw that the very fact of change of relationships in land ownership and social stability in the countryside held enormous revolutionary promise. In Lenin's view, if Stolypin was creating a class of successful peasant farmers, then there must come into being a still larger class of increasingly poor and deprived peasants. From this he deduced that the sole solution for the mass of the peasantry, if they were not either to perish or to be driven from the land altogether, was a mass peasant uprising, which the Social Democrats must struggle to promote.

During these years Russian Social Democracy was hopelessly divided and in perpetual conflict. Parallel conferences of factions took place repeatedly, each claiming to represent true opinion. Yet there still existed a continuing movement towards reconciliation and unification. It expressed the Social Democratic element in the Russian revolutionary tradition: the desire to create and develop a mass party. Though this goal was remote indeed, attempts were made to present a more coherent leadership as a prerequisite for success among the masses.

An All-Russian Conference which took place in Paris in January

1909 mustered a mere sixteen voting delegates: five Bolsheviks, three Mensheviks, five Polish Social Democrats, and three *Bundists*. Lenin used this occasion to secure a formal condemnation of both the Bolshevik 'recallists' and the Menshevik 'liquidators'.

In January 1910 all the factions and groups of the party met in Paris for a conference of the Central Committee. Fourteen voting delegates attended, including Bolsheviks, Mensheviks, Polish Social Democrats, Letts, the *Bund*, and a dissident Bolshevik group called *Vperedists*, after the newspaper they published (*Forward*). In addition, there were non-voting representatives of the party Central Organ, *Sotsial-Demokrat* (Lenin); the Bolshevik factional paper *Proletarii* (Kamenev); the Menshevik factional paper *Golos Sotsial-Demokrata* (Martov); and finally Trotsky, who was most active in attempting to unite the party by means of the voluntary disbanding of all factions, and who represented his own small non-factional group, which published its paper, *Pravda*, in Vienna.

In an apparent spirit of reconciliation the January meetings of the Central Committee achieved an illusory agreement to disband the factions and discontinue rival publications. A united editorial board, consisting of Lenin, Zinoviev, Martov, Dan and a Polish representative, was to publish the party organ *Sotsial-Demokrat*. The assembly also adopted a number of decisions which were meant to resolve doctrinal and tactical differences between the various factions and splinter groups. Thus it castigated all forms of extremism in the party, including the left-wing 'recallists' and the right-wing 'liquidators'. In an attempt to unite 'all and sundry', the Mensheviks succeeded in getting approval for an invitation to the 'liquidators' to take part in the illegal Central Committee in Russia. At the same time the conference recognised the legitimacy of Trotsky's group as well as the Bolshevik *Vpered* group, and they were encouraged to continue their activities as components of the party as a whole.

But no amount of conciliatory feeling could hide the fact that, whatever bodies and offices the party set up in apparent unity, it was invariably on a factional basis that they were compelled to appoint members. The pattern of the Central Committee itself was applied to all party organs, a plain recognition that factional interests would continue.

Lenin's attitude to the new climate was unmistakably contemptuous. Unity had always had a special connotation for him when it was the slogan and creation of others: it meant the good-humoured, flabby lack of resolve and 'trading in principles' that a sinking of past differences implied, and it presaged doom. Unification of 'all and sundry' meant to him the contamination of the pure, and it was a foregone conclusion that he would not long associate with such 'unity'. The Menshevik olive-branch to the 'liquidators' was bad enough; far worse was the latters' refusal to be tempted back into the limbo of illegality and what they knew to be Lenin's projected sphere of influence.[9] It was this 'mess' that gave Lenin the pretext on which to start fighting again. Now he resolved that this unity must be dispersed and the only proper unity, that of a vigorous Bolshevik apparatus under his single control, must take its place.

His hostility was the greater for his having been forced through a personal ordeal. For it was at the Paris conference that the party as a whole had learned of his direct involvement in the great Tiflis robbery of 1907, and in consequence he had been forced to agree to burn the remaining banknotes. Also at the Paris Conference the episode of the Schmidt inheritance came to light and again Lenin had to agree to place the funds in the discretionary hands of three German trustees, Kautsky, Mehring and Klara Zetkin, though it would take eighteen months of intrigue, pressure and scandal to make him hand over even a part of the money. The fact that both factions may have wanted to control these funds for their own purposes did not diminish the propaganda value to the Mensheviks of Lenin's moral negligence.

In order to effect a final break Lenin resorted to his customary technique. His own agents, illegally despatched to Russia, were to establish their own commission and prepare the ground for a party conference. Throughout 1911 Lenin conducted his preparations. His aim, of convening a meeting that would proclaim

Bolshevik principles and Bolshevik institutions in the name of the entire party, was greatly helped by the calculating intervention of the Tsarist secret police. Minutely informed by their own agents in the Bolshevik organisation, the police recognised in Lenin a wedge that would, they hoped, maintain the forces of Social Democracy in permanent dislocation and impotence.

Thus they ensured that, while Bolsheviks who were working for conciliation were arrested, Lenin's agents preparing for his conference were left in peace to complete their task.[10] Yet Lenin's Russian Organising Commission failed almost totally to gain recognition among the local committees, even as representative of the Bolshevik faction, and as a result the 'party' conference which convened in Prague in January 1912 was representative of no more than the fourteen voting delegates who attended it. Protests against calling the meeting a party conference were ignored by the Leninist majority, who went on to proclaim it the 'All-party Conference of the RSDRP, and the supreme organ of the party'. The legend is compounded in Soviet nomenclature as the 'Sixth (Prague) All-Russian Conference of the RSDRP'.

A new Central Committee was elected, comprising seven picked Bolsheviks including Lenin and his closest associate, Grigory Zinoviev, and one Roman Malinovsky, who was later to be exposed as a police spy.

In April 1912, having persuaded the Central Committee to withdraw its subsidy to Trotsky's *Pravda*, Lenin began to publish his own legal newspaper for the Russian workers. He appropriated the name of Trotsky's paper, *Pravda*, in the expectation that he would thus acquire the substantial good-will that it had built up. Lenin's policy was now to enter the same arena of legal operations as the Mensheviks and the 'Liquidators' and to rival them for the allegiance of the workers. Influence over the legal labour movement and trade unions was to be achieved by clandestine cells under party control, which would be ready to direct the massed workers when the moment of insurrection returned. Lenin's renewed vigorous and attacking policy provoked his opponents to greater efforts at uniting their own forces.

But however mythical Lenin's claims to represent party opinion were, his opponents were not, nor it seems ever would be, sufficiently aggressive to compete with him for the new, and psychologically crucial, party titles that he had once again arrogated to his own faction. In August 1912, Trotsky, the most active 'unifier', and the leading Mensheviks, organised a conference in Vienna which gave rise to a new configuration known as the August Bloc. All shades of opinion attended, except that the Polish Social Democrats and Plekhanov were not represented, and Lenin did not deign to attend 'their' conference. Among the non-Leninist Bolsheviks who did attend was one from Moscow who was in fact a police spy and whose secret assignment was to disrupt the proceedings.

Far more representative of party opinion than Lenin's 'All-party Conference', the August meeting nonetheless described itself as no more than it really was, a 'Conference of RSDRP Organisations'. And, still on the defensive against Lenin, it called its Central Committee by the ephemeral title of Organising Committee. The extent of this error of judgement would fully emerge when, in competing with the Mensheviks for the workers' support, Lenin would be able to speak from the 'official' platform, while the Mensheviks would have to expend their energies in staking their claim to legitimacy. Moreover, the very range of the 'August Bloc' and the endemic dissidence of Russian socialists soon rendered the combination sterile as an organisational entity, and negligible as an apparatus to compare with the Bolsheviks.

In spite of these defects in the Menshevik leadership and in spite of the competitive attitude of the Bolsheviks, when the two factions fought the elections to the Fourth Duma, in September 1912, the Mensheviks gained seven and the Bolsheviks six seats. Such a nearly equal result was possible because the campaign was fought on a non-factional basis and, indeed, the workers were reluctant to distinguish Bolshevik from Menshevik. As well as the Mensheviks, any Bolsheviks, including most of the Bolshevik Duma deputies, would also have welcomed unity.

The relative autonomy of the Duma Social Democrats made it possible for them to give some rein to these feelings, and at the end of 1912 the two Duma groups agreed that they would henceforth act in accord. To his intense annoyance Lenin now found that the editors of *Pravda* (Stalin and Molotov) were making judicious cuts in his articles in order to attenuate his anti-Menshevik tone. Lenin acted quickly to open the eyes of both *Pravda* and 'his' deputies and to redirect their view towards what they must consider their proper goal: a split in the Duma group and the separate conduct of the two factions within the Duma. The means at his disposal for effecting this strategem are more a comment on the regime that covertly abetted him than they are on Lenin, for he at any rate had never concealed duplicity as a valuable weapon.

Roman Malinovsky entered Lenin's ranks at the Prague Conference of 1912, where he also met his leader for the first time.* He was already a salaried agent of the Tsarist secret police, which he had been serving certainly since 1909. His activities, apart from a criminal past, had to date consisted of organising and running the Petersburg Metal Workers' Union, where he diligently pursued the legal work of the good Menshevik he was then thought to be. Simultaneously, however, he abetted the interests of the state by withstanding Lenin's attempts to infiltrate his union, which, it seemed to the police, would involve a return to the old habits of the illegal underground. When the movement towards unity in the party seemed near success, Malinovsky was instructed to turn Bolshevik, and to work for a position close to Lenin. The unity of the party was fought against by the police, who observed that as long as the factions were mutually hostile the police could more easily keep them in their present state of impotence. And since Lenin was working tirelessly towards total disruption the police naturally sought to help him.

* For the fullest and most penetrating account of this episode see Bertram D. Wolfe, *Three Who Made a Revolution*, Chapter 21, on which this summary leans.

The policy of infiltrating agents into the Social Democratic party continued in spite of the great repercussions of the Socialist Revolutionary-Azef scandal in 1909. As long as the masses were quiescent the police calculated that the risk of further scandals was worth the opportunity to manipulate the levers of control at the very summit of the party. Thus in both factions police agents were helped to high positions of trust by the judicious and well-planned removal of local leaders. The Malinovsky card turned out to be an ace of trumps.

Lenin was enormously impressed by Malinovsky's energy and experience as a workers' leader. He put him up to run as a Social Democrat candidate for the elections to the Fourth Duma, and the police used their good offices to cover up Malinovsky's criminal past, which should have disqualified him. His candidacy was also safeguarded by the timely arrest of local contenders. His election was greeted by the police with a ten-fold increase in his salary, and by Lenin with his appointment as Duma spokesman for the Bolsheviks. The Social Democrat group as a whole chose him as its vice-chairman, with the Menshevik Chkheidze as chairman.

Malinovsky's role in the Duma was doubled by the police spy Chernomazov who became editor of the Bolshevik *Pravda*, in May 1913. Its conciliatory editor, Stalin, had been arrested in March as a direct result of a Malinovsky stratagem. Chernomazov followed Lenin's 'splitting' line until February 1914, when he was 'unmasked' by a police move calculated to deflect growing attention to Malinovsky.

By late 1913, however, Malinovsky and Lenin had succeeded in their common task, and the Social Democrat group in the Duma had been split into its factional components, with the six Bolsheviks claiming equal voice with the seven Mensheviks. Suspicion, which had existed from the very beginning of Malinovsky's Bolshevik career, was mounting rapidly. Now that his police role, of splitting the Duma group, was accomplished it was important for the police to reduce his stature as a spokesman of revolution. Also the mounting suspicion threatened to undo his police work, for nothing welded the factions so well as the discovery of sabotage. Therefore, in May 1914 Malinovsky suddenly, and without prior notice to anyone, resigned from the Duma on orders from the police, giving health reasons as his excuse.

He went to Lenin, who was living at Cracow, close to the Russian frontier. There he spun a yarn that his sudden resignation had been forced upon him by the police who threatened to expose him as a rapist. The rumours about Malinovsky that Lenin had previously succeeded in silencing, with threats of fire and brimstone, sprang to life with a vengeance and Lenin again vehemently defended his 'wonderful workers' leader'. The Mensheviks demanded a full party tribunal to examine the case. The possible outcome would have been more disastrous to Lenin than to the regime, and he evidently recognised this, for he evaded the Menshevik demand by forming a tribunal of his own.

The tribunal consisted of Lenin, Zinoviev and another 'man of trust', Hanecki-Fürstenberg. It could not have been a less impartial body had it included Malinovsky himself. The culprit was exonerated and, as it was Lenin's habit to attack when cornered, the 'tribunal' attacked the Mensheviks as treacherous calumniators. Malinovsky was admonished in the Bolshevik press for abandoning his post, and expelled from the party. During the First World War he was praised by the Bolsheviks for the valuable work he was doing, under German auspices, to spread revolutionary propaganda among Russian prisoners-of-war. When he returned to Russia in November 1918, however, his full story had already been exposed by the opening of the police archives under the Provisional Government. Nonetheless Malinovsky demanded a hearing with Lenin's testimony. Lenin remained personally aloof, but a trial took place and Malinovsky was duly shot.

In 1914, Lenin made great public showing of his trust in Malinovsky and in his alibi.* However, the possibility that the rumours were true alarmed him seriously. He wrote to Inessa

* Wolfe, *op. cit.*, p. 553, accepts Lenin's arguments and self-defence as reasonable.

Armand (in English); 'Very improbable but we are obliged to control all "ouï-dire" . . . You can easily imagine how much I am worried.'[11] A letter which he wrote to another Bolshevik deputy, in the early summer of 1914 when an investigation by the Socialist International was pending, reveals what he really felt about the man he so ardently defended. 'We've finished with Malinovsky, it's all over. He's dead, suicide. No good nagging on about it and wasting time. To work, and down with the gutter journalists!'[12] Malinovsky, though politically 'dead', was in reality enjoying the 6,000-rouble retirement bonus his police chiefs had given him, and still very capable of compromising Lenin.

In the summer of 1914 the Socialist International intervened in the factional discord of the Russian party, offering its good offices as mediator. Lenin who was 'extremely nervous, almost ill'[13] would not attend the hearings in Brussels, but sent instead his confidante and friend, Inessa Armand. He impressed upon her that the Bolshevik 'autonomous party' would not have its hands tied by any outside agency. She was to treat the International Bureau, which conducted the hearing, as no more than a mediator whose function was 'to convey to the enemy: (1) our *terms* and (2) the *objective facts*, and that's all!!'[14]

The conference produced a resolution which was as conciliatory as Lenin could have expected. It found that the differences within the Russian Social Democratic party were not substantial enough to hamper unity, and it called for unity on the basis of the party programme. A general unification congress should take place, and the minority must accept the view of the majority. The double irony here was that Lenin had no intention as the minority of accepting the views of the majority, much less the exhortations of 'that fool Kautsky', the chairman at the Socialist International hearing. He had already set in train the preparations for yet another, final, 'party' congress at which the separate, autonomous existence of the Bolshevik party was to be proclaimed once and for all. In the event, both the projected 'unification' and the Bolshevik congress were forestalled by the outbreak of the First World War.

8

The End of the Monarchy

The mood of political protest which had permeated society on the eve of the war with Japan was, by the time of the First World War, felt only in the sphere of the political parties. The socialists had been heartened, in 1912, by a new surge of strike activity, but in the overwhelming majority of incidents the issue was economic, further confirmation of both the relative prosperity of the country and the state of mind of the working class. Strikes were on the whole only staged when it was recognised that something could be gained.

During the Russo-Japanese war, defeatist sentiments had been common among intellectuals and professional men, while the masses had remained completely indifferent. When the First World War broke out, however, defeatism was a sentiment felt only by the extreme left, and expressed solely in the European exile. Following upon the enthusiastic demonstrations of patriotism with which the workers and society at large greeted the Tsar's announcement of general mobilisation, there followed at least two years during which the prevalent feeling in Russia was the desire for a successful war policy leading to a glorious victory. Economic progress and the gradual but certain benefits being derived from the reforms were the basis of the popularity of the war. At the same time, the greater feeling of physical nearness to the war and the much greater involvement of the population than in the war with Japan, meant that as never before the gaze of the nation would be focussed on the government, judging the efforts it was making to defend the country and promote victory. Public interest was facilitated by the numerous popular newspapers that had sprung up after 1905, under the less stringent censorship. News now travelled fast and there were many more people interested in it. Politicians need no longer go to street corners or factory gates to get the attention of the public, when a newspaper column would serve to reach a much wider audience.

The Duma was in recess when war was declared. A one-day session on 8 August was the occasion of a patriotic demonstration by the deputies. Only the Social Democrats, for once united, were outright in their condemnation of the war and in their refusal to vote for war credits, though to no effect.* The Duma was adjourned for six months, and a spate of emergency legislation was issued by decree.

Having itself ensured that the Duma was an institution without power or authority, the government acted with consistency in now precluding the public's elected representatives from taking an active part in the defence of the country. But its action, though consistent, was blind. Relations between the regime and the leaders of the opposition parties, never cordial, were now openly distrustful. Nothing proved this more ostentatiously than the government's neglect of the Duma's show of loyalty in July. The government's view was that the business of war, like the business of government, must be conducted by those who knew their responsibilities to the fatherland and not by power-hungry politicians.

Thus the budget, which even before the war had been only partially debated in the Duma, was now hidden from its view. Similarly, although the government recognised the valuable contribution which the zemstvos and municipalities could make to the war effort, and indeed made full use of that contribution,

* This subject will be dealt with in greater detail in the following chapter.

yet no attempt was made to channel it through the Duma. The attitude of the Tsar himself played an important part here. Ill at ease with political issues and questions of reform, he was refreshed by the simplicity and sacredness of purpose which he saw in war. For the first and probably the only time in his life, Nicolas felt like the autocrat he thought he ought to be. With the knowledge and advice of only the Council of Ministers he personally issued a mass of legislation.

The Duma was recalled for a three-day session on 9 February 1915, during which the party leaders were assured in secret that the army was well provided for and that the Duma need not concern itself about the cost. In fact the Duma had found outlets of its own. The day after its one-day session in July 1914 the Duma had met privately and agreed to set up a committee for the relief of the wounded and of families of the dead. Meeting twice a week, and composed of any deputies who chanced to be in Petrograd,* the committee soon became the natural substitute for the Duma itself. Questions raised turned increasingly on the government's conduct of the war: the shortage of supplies, the Russian retreat from Galicia, and the profound consequences of the German occupation of Russian Poland. The deputies received no answers to these questions, since they had been excluded from the government's plans, and not surprisingly they convinced themselves that the government had no answers to give. Not only did they doubt the government's abilities, but they, rightly, believed that they could help. Mutual distrust and scepticism formed the background to all government–Duma relations during this last phase of their coexistence.

The early experiences of the war did nothing to arouse faith in the government. The Russian army and navy had been reorganised after the defeats in 1905 and considerable modernisation had taken place. But, like her allies, Russia was badly prepared for combat

* Petersburg was translated into its Slavonic form after the outbreak of war.

with a war machine as efficient as Germany's. Russia's first campaign, in East Prussia during August 1914, undertaken at the urgent request of her allies to divert German pressure in Belgium and France, proved disastrous. Lack of coordination, inept command, inadequate supplies, led to the total surrender of two army corps and the suicide of an army commander, General Samsonov. In the course of the summer of 1915 Russia lost all her western strongholds and new and serious difficulties arose in the rear.

Since the beginning of the war whole areas of the empire had been placed under military command, and the economy of these areas was hastily geared to military needs. As the army took first priority on all goods and services, severe shortages arose in these areas. Military control of communications interrupted the flow of goods between town and country. In the village, where there was now more money to spend, manufactured goods were at a premium, while agricultural supplies to the towns suffered similarly. These effects worsened as the burden of the war increased with the progress of time.

The government's financial problems were enormous. It met the immense cost of the war not through increased taxation, but by huge foreign loans and the issue of paper money, which rapidly fell in value as the volume of banknotes in circulation multiplied.* Russia's economic health had for over thirty years been based on a favourable trade balance with foreign countries, principally Germany. Large grain exports had paid for the modern machinery which she imported to exploit her rich natural resources, and these were in turn applied to the further expansion of Russian industry. This foreign trade was drastically affected by the war. Russia's main trade routes were through the Black Sea and the Baltic. Both these outlets were shut off by the war, although neutral Sweden would continue to play an important part as Russia's bridge to nominally closed markets.[1] Vladivostok, the only outlet still open, was too far from the market to justify the enormous cost of transporting consumer goods across

* By 1916 the rouble had fallen to thirty-nine per cent of its pre-war value.

the whole continent, and was used instead as an importing centre for military material from the Allies. In brief, Russia's trade balance was converted from a surplus in 1913 to a loss, by the end of the war, twenty times greater than that surplus. This change was felt at home in terms of higher prices and fewer goods.

As military setbacks and economic dislocation in the rear mounted, the Duma Relief Committee made increasingly desperate demands for an effective part of the nation's war effort to be placed in Duma hands. While drawing attention to the government's inefficiencies, this agitation also implied condemnation of the regime as a whole, and fostered a widespread demand for a 'government enjoying the nation's trust'. The campaign, conducted in zemstvos and city councils, had gathered enough volume by the summer of 1915 for it to be supported by a majority of the Council of Ministers. At this juncture, the nation's leadership underwent an unexpected change.

Since the beginning of the war the Tsar had been fully engaged in military affairs, visiting the fronts and inspecting the troops, and in general giving support to his staff, but being in what he later called a false position, without real authority.[2] At the same time he had maintained working contact with his ministers, and carried out his state functions. Now in August 1915, against the urgent advice of ten of his twelve ministers, and precisely at the lowest ebb of Russia's military fortunes, he replaced his uncle, the Grand Duke Nikolai Nikolaevich, as the Supreme Commander. It was an act of personal identification with his country's destiny, which itself bore directly on the fate of the dynasty. Victory would strengthen the throne, while defeat would further the cause of revolution.

With his new responsibilities the Tsar came to rely more heavily on the work which his wife was eager to do for him: interviewing the ministers and in general keeping him in touch with affairs in the capital. At the end of August 1915 he wrote to her: 'What a pity that you have not been fulfilling this duty [until now]'.[3] The Empress became a positive fountain of information, rumours, scandal, gossip and patronage. She had a word for every conceivable item of concern to the government of the country. Her likes and dislikes were frequently based on her protectiveness towards Rasputin who was already a target of many critics. And often she would cite his words as added persuasion for some preference which she wanted to urge upon Nicolas.

More dangerously for the regime, she took it upon herself to attack the government's critics. She wrote to Nicolas at the end of August 1915: 'They need a sharp answer, to mind their own business . . . nobody needs their opinion. . . . I shall tell the old man [the President of the Council of Ministers] I have no patience with these meddlesome chatterboxes.'[4] Equally, she had little time for the ministers who, showing their own minds, had opposed Nicolas's decision to assume the supreme command. 'I long to thrash nearly all the ministers', she wrote.[5] She persisted in pressing the Tsar to make changes in the cabinet and in the course of 1915–16 seven of the original ten rebellious ministers were removed. It is hard to assess the degree to which the Tsar's mind was actually changed by her interference, and it is true that on several occasions he asserted his own views positively against her advice even though it was supported by their Friend. In spite of this, her constant, daily, concern with government matters, and the capriciousness of her judgements (she was evidently an hysterical woman) was an unstable influence on affairs of state and exposed the regime to further attacks.

Though everything in her letters points to the contrary, the Empress became the object of ominous whisperings concerning the settlement of a separate peace with the Germans, which she was supposed to be negotiating through her German relatives. The intimacy which Rasputin was alleged to enjoy in the royal household gave rise to still further rumours of breaches in state security. But whenever the Tsar let her into military secrets he emphatically enjoined her to tell nobody, to 'keep it to *yourself*'.[6] When, in September 1916, she gave Nicolas a long account of Rasputin's opinions on a series of important state matters, including new ministerial candidates,[7] the Tsar replied:

'Our Friend's opinions of people are sometimes very strange, as you know yourself—therefore one must be careful, especially with appointments to high offices.'[8]

From the beginning of 1916, when the new cabinet was formed, there ensued what came to be known as the game of ministerial leapfrog, with a dizzy succession of ministers, each one less capable and less likely to succeed than the last. Nicolas wrote (in the same letter): 'All these changes make my head go round. In my opinion, they are too frequent. In any case they are not good for the internal situation of the country, as each new man brings with him alterations to the administration.' He might have added that they put weapons into the hands of the government's critics.

The hostility which both the Tsar and the Empress felt for the Duma politicians found particular expression in a personal hatred of Guchkov, leader of the Octobrists and one-time president of the Duma. The Empress wrote[9] in January 1916: 'Gutchkov is very ill—wish he would go to yonder world for you and Russians blessing . . .'* Guchkov had been involved in a political scandal around the name of Rasputin in 1912 and had then earned the Empress's everlasting enmity. Since the summer of 1915 he had come into prominence as the driving force in the Central War Industries Committee.

This 'public', non-government, body came into being as a result of meetings between industrialists and businessmen earlier in 1915. Its main aims were the conversion of factories to war production and to supervise the coordination of all commerce and industry to achieve this. By the end of 1915 there were twenty-eight provincial branches. Their members were representatives of industry, commerce, government, the Union of Zemstvos and Municipalities (*Zemgor* in its Russian abbreviation), and most notably of labour. *Zemgor* set up a joint committee for the purpose of placing orders from the Ministry of War and coordinating their execution. At the same time the government

* The translation is probably inferior to the Empress's own English style.

itself set up Special Councils composed of public figures and civil servants to deal with national defence, transport, food and fuel supplies. The government thus recognised that the poor record of the first year of the war warranted its accepting help from the public or voluntary organisations.

The Empress, however, regarded the War Industries Committee and its counterparts as usurpers of the royal prerogative. Her letters to the Tsar are full of bitter and angry vituperation against the ministers who had allowed Guchkov, whom she wished to see hanged, to go so far. She wrote: 'I wish you could shut up that rotten War Industries Committee altogether.' In the same way she continually tried to persuade the Tsar also to abolish the Duma. She constantly urged Nicolas to show his autocratic power, not to let the ministers rule him, not to let busybodies from the Duma take over the tasks which only he, as Emperor, was fit to carry out. The repetitious replacement of ministers who either showed initiative, or held opinions, or were tolerant towards the initiative of public figures, owed much to her possessive conception of a Tsar's role.

But the efforts of the public bodies soon yielded results and military supplies began to increase, albeit at the considerable cost involved in running a duplicate administration. An impressive feature of the War Industries Committee, and one which only added to the Empress's displeasure, was the fact that for the first time representatives of both industry and labour met together to discuss the nation's production problems.

The attitude of the revolutionary parties towards participating in the Committees was of course varied. The Bolsheviks repudiated them, and exhorted the workers to overthrow Tsarism, not to help it survive by supporting the war effort: only in defeat and dissolution of the empire could the workers expect to see hope of their socialist revolution. Bolshevik practice, however, as we shall see in the next chapter, was far from official doctrine. The Mensheviks were divided, the group which favoured supporting the war as a defence against Prussian militarism, also favouring participation in the War Industries Committees. The

majority of Socialist Revolutionaries were of the same mind. At
the end of November 1915 ten labour representatives were
elected to the Central War Industries Committee. The secret
police who, like Lenin, had revolution on their minds night and
day, made sure that one of the labour representatives, Abrosimov,
was an agent of theirs.

In July 1915 the Duma was recalled and the campaign for
including public figures in the government, 'a government
enjoying national confidence', gathered momentum. A united
front of about 300 deputies came into being in the course of that
summer, ranging from the Kadets to the moderate nationalists,
and including members of the State Council. It became known as
the Progressive Bloc and, although its nucleus consisted of men
with decisively progressive views, most of its members were
moderates, whose chief aim was to bring an end to the gulf that
existed between the government and the parliament in order to
facilitate effective conduct of the war. The programme of the
Progressive Bloc, in addition to the demand for a government
enjoying the confidence of the nation, called for the removal of
restrictions on public initiative, limitation of military discipline
over the civilian population, abolition of religious and national
discrimination, greater freedom for the trade unions, for the
zemstvos and the municipalities, and an amnesty of all political
and religious prisoners, being held without trial.[10]

The Progressive Bloc was in effect demanding no less than a
major change of outlook from the government as a prerequisite
for the successful conduct of the war. Out of the specifically
permitted activities in which they sought to engage, and against
a background of more lenient government they anticipated a
reformed regime which would continue in being after the end of
the war. The programme, which was formulated at the same time
as the Tsar assumed the supreme command, had the support of
most of the ministers. This 'revolt' of the cabinet, compounded
by their refusal to endorse the Tsar's new functions, incensed the
Empress, who made it her first task to remove them and find men

with views more congenial to her taste. She pressed the Tsar to reject the programme and this he did, on 16 September 1915. Moreover he prorogued the Duma and set no date for its reassembly.

Whether she realised it or not, the Empress set the preservation of the autocratic principle above the survival of the country. The scars of 1905 were deep on her mind, and she could no longer distinguish between the benefit of public initiative and the spoils of the opposition parties seeking power. And to a great extent neither could the politicians. If the Empress believed that the politicians were merely using the war as a vehicle to power, then the opposition at least recognised in the war the opportunity for winning the right to govern. It thus came down to a struggle, between the Progressive Bloc and those in the government and administration under the Empress's hand, as to who in Russia was to win the war. The Empress made herself the target of the Progressive Bloc, and the fatal chink in her armour was Rasputin.

It was ironic that during 1916 Russia's war efforts were rewarded by some spectacular successes, while the popular enthusiasm that should have been harnessed to consolidate these gains was dissipated in the conflict between the Empress and 'society', as the opposition liked to represent itself. In February 1916 the Duma was convened again, amid a clamour of indignation against the rumoured influence of Rasputin. In March the Duma was stunned by the news that Polivanov, the Minister of War and almost the only man in the government still enjoying some popularity, had been replaced by a total nonentity, Shuvaev. During the summer of 1916 a brilliant campaign by General Brusilov on the Galician front confirmed the value of cooperation between the public bodies and the military administration. But the enthusiasm roused by this success, itself of little strategic value, was short-lived. The dislocation of the rear was worsening and making itself felt where, politically, it mattered most—the capital. Fear that food and fuel would be short in the coming winter was echoed by speeches in the Duma calling with an ever more desperate voice for 'sanity' in the government.

As winter approached, socialist propaganda in the capital was stepped up, more frequent and more massive strikes occurred calling for alleviation of the unbearable burden of the war. Seizing on any convenient slogan to express pent-up anger, the workers began shouting that first of all it was necessary to get rid of the 'Germans at home' before fighting the Germans abroad. The reference was to the Empress's German origin and to that of her new President of the Council of Ministers, Stürmer, who in January had replaced the ancient Goremykin. Stürmer, who was favoured by Rasputin, was also made Foreign Minister in June 1916, a post especially unsuitable for this unintelligent narrow bureaucrat, known to be corrupt and sycophantic. His appointment enraged even extreme conservatives and dismayed the Allied military representatives in Russia. The opposition campaign against the Empress's interference in state affairs and the malevolent presence of Rasputin in high places, was coming to a climax. 'Dark forces' were said to be acting in Germany's interests, and the 'hand of the enemy' was said to be influencing the course of state affairs.

In November 1916 these rumours were expressed in a long speech delivered in the Duma by Milyukov, leader of the Kadets. Later reported under the title 'Storm Signal', the speech, and the motives underlying it, was seen by the right as the signal for the storm to begin, and by the left as the signal that the storm was coming. Milyukov drew a picture of Russia's plight as a country led in war by a gang of incompetents whose stupidity was so manifest that even the Germans could welcome their appointment to office. Their mistakes and ineptitudes amounted *in effect* to treason. 'When the Duma reminds [the government] with increasing persistence that the rear must be organised for a successful war, and the government goes on insisting that to organise means to organise the revolution, and consciously prefers chaos and lack of organisation—what is that, stupidity or treason?' He repeated this formula several times, in the context of other issues, and when a right-wing deputy, Markov, called out, 'And what is your speech, stupidity or treason?' Milyukov replied, 'My speech is a service to the fatherland ....'

In essence, Milyukov summarised, society was dissatisfied with the present government on two counts, incompetence and ill-will. In conclusion he stated, on behalf of the Duma majority, that the people would only support a government which properly understood its business, which was willing to implement the programme of the Progressive Bloc, and which would seek support for every aspect of its work among the Duma majority.[11]

This, and other critical speeches by Duma deputies, were reprinted in thousands of copies and circulated throughout the empire, most notably appearing in the front-line trenches. The effect was as devastating as the opposition intended it to be. Milyukov's speech was the culmination of a whole series of attacks on the government, personified by the Empress and by implication Rasputin, which the opposition had conducted for over a year, so it was not surprising that the popular response was great. Nor was it surprising that the speech was felt to express what many people had been wanting to say. It conveniently focussed national discontent.

The immediate response of the government was to dismiss Stürmer as a liability. At last the right wing saw the danger to the monarchy from Rasputin's alleged and widely believed malevolent influence. To save the monarchy the right wing appealed to the government to beg the Tsar for Rasputin's removal. Their voices were joined by those of state councillors, the high nobility, and the British and French Ambassadors, but all without effect. Finally at the end of December a small group consisting of the Grand Duke Dmitri Pavlovich, a nephew of the Tsar, the young Prince Felix Yusupov, and a right-wing deputy V. M. Purish-kevich, conspired to murder Rasputin as a desperate measure to neutralise the opposition's offensive against the regime.

The exaggeration of Rasputin's influence was proved by the fact that nothing changed as a result of his removal. The Empress, though grieved, continued her work as before. His so-called guidance had been no more than the holy sanction for actions which she herself devised, and he had been too much the charlatan to allow his judgement to conflict with hers. The Tsar made no response to the intensified appeals of leading figures, when Rasputin's removal was seen to have had no effect.

Shortly after, the Duma was adjourned. The Progressive Bloc now drew up plans for a more drastic solution, the abdication of the Tsar in favour of his son, with his brother Michael as regent. At this stage nothing more was done. On 6 February 1917, the militant tone of the Duma majority was taken up by the labour group in the War Industries Committee, which issued a call to the workers of the capital to come out *en masse* on the day of the Duma's reassembly.[12] But on 12 February the entire group was arrested. In the event the demonstration, whose aim was to declare support for the Duma and thus generate a revolutionary situation, did not take place because of disagreements between the Bolsheviks and Mensheviks.

On 27 February the Duma was recalled. The situation in the capital was described by deputies as critical. The winter was unusually cold and both fuel and food were in ever-decreasing supply. Economic demands from the workers were now aligned with political pressure. To an agitated Duma, Kerensky, leader of the Labour–Socialist Revolutionary group in the Duma and privy to the plan to secure an abdication, declared that now was the time to get rid of the Tsar, by assassination if necessary. But no action was taken, either by the opposition to further this plan, or by the government to suppress its instigator. The bread queues lengthened and strikes increased in size and number. On 8 March there were disturbances in the bread queues which quickly spread into the centre of the city and the industrial suburbs. Police and troops kept the crowds in check and the only damage done was to some bakeries. The crowds were joined by the large number of workers who, by coincidence, had been locked out of the great Putilov factory the day before, over a labour dispute. Their militancy heated the mood of the masses.

Massive strikes of up to 200,000 workers took place again on the following day, 9 March, this time with a concerted attempt to carry the demonstration into the centre of the city. Although the crowd made some attacks on the police, with stones and chunks of ice, no shots were fired, and more important, the Cossack detachments, traditional scourge of any street protest meetings, refrained from action and even appeared to be on the side of the mob. By the following day, 10 March, the city was in the grip of a general strike. That evening the Tsar, who had been at the General Headquarters since 7 March, telegraphed the military commandant of the city, General Khabalov, 'I order you to suppress all disorders in the capital tomorrow, as they are intolerable at this difficult time of war with Germany and Austria.'[13]

By using arms on the crowds, and by arresting a large number of socialist agitators and leaders, including four of the Bolshevik Petrograd Committee, Khabalov believed that he had taken all necessary steps to ensure order. But a more important development had already come into play which would quickly render this confidence void. The city housed some 200,000 troops, of whom a large part were new recruits, and old hands convalescing from the trenches. Neither category was reliable and both had been subjected to revolutionary agitation. On the evening of the 11th mutiny broke out in one company, but was quickly quelled. The virus of mutiny was, however, at large and by the following morning almost every section of the garrison had been infected and was seething in revolt.

On 12 March the situation reached its crisis, for not only were thousands of strikers massed once again on the streets, but now they were joined by armed troops, who had 'gone over to the revolution'. They occupied the arsenals and the Peter-Paul Fortress, released prisoners from gaol, including the recently arrested labour group of the War Industries Committee, and by the morning of the next day the city was in their hands.

On the same day the majority in the Duma, which the Tsar had ordered to adjourn on the previous evening, resolved to take matters into their own hands. They virtually repudiated the prorogation order by reassembling as a private body. They established a Provisional Committee to meet the desperate situation in the capital: the prospect of a total breakdown in production and army discipline threatened far worse than the almost forgotten war.

Also on 12 March there was set up, in urgent emulation of 1905, a Provisional Executive Committee of the Soviet of Workers' Deputies, composed at first of left-wing Duma deputies, trade-union men and the released members of the labour group of the War Industries Committee. Since the focus of public attention was the Duma itself, the new Soviet took up its place in the Tauride Palace, where the Duma Committee was meeting. Its first meeting was markedly militant with large numbers of armed soldiers in evidence. Renamed the Soviet of Workers' and Soldiers' Deputies, this new organ of potentially great authority undertook first to alleviate those burdens which had brought about the situation, namely food and fuel shortages.

In Moscow events were following a similar course: a Provisional Revolutionary Committee was established, and the troops of the garrison came steadily over to the workers on general strike and the revolutionary crowds. In the capital the political shape of the revolution was emerging. On 15 March the Duma Committee proclaimed itself, at last, the Provisional Government, and the dual power, consisting on the one hand of the armed forces of the Soviet, and on the other of the self-constituted caretaker government, now came into being.

The authority of the former government had evaporated by 13 March, when its members were either arrested, or hiding at home 'praying for a frost cold enough to freeze the workers off the streets'. Nicolas II, still at GHQ, persistently refused to heed the desperate telegrams coming from the President of the Duma, Rodzyanko. Nothing could overcome the deep distrust he felt for such 'public figures'. Finally realising the seriousness of the crisis, Nicolas left Mogilev for the capital on the morning of 13 March. But hearing that the railway line to the capital was in the hands of revolutionary troops, the Tsar's staff persuaded him to proceed to the Northern HQ at Pskov instead, and there, it was hoped, to collect loyal support before going on to the capital, where he was anxious to join his family.

Arriving at Pskov on 14 March Nicolas was met by his senior generals with an urgent appeal to grant a constitution and representative government. He conceded, and cabled the President of the Duma permission to form a government. At this stage Nicolas still believed that it was possible to establish a constitutional monarchy. So did the Provisional Committee, for on 15 March it sent two deputies, Shulgin and Guchkov, to Pskov in order to persuade Nicolas to abdicate in favour of his son, with the Grand Duke Michael as regent. The Tsar had already decided to abdicate, convinced by messages from his general staff, but when he heard that the Duma emissaries were coming he decided that he would not place his beloved son at the mercy of a 'constitutional' government formed by his much despised enemies in the Duma. He therefore abdicated on 15 March in favour of his brother, Grand Duke Michael.

Some members of the Provisional Committee were firmly of the opinion that constitutional monarchy was the best form of government for Russia in time of war. They feared that any more radical change of system would completely disrupt the war effort. But when the two emissaries returned to the capital and announced the good news to crowds at the railway station they quickly realised that a change of monarch would not find wide support. When the members of the Provisional Committee met at Grand Duke Michael's residence on the morning of 16 March most of them were now of the opinion that he would be a singularly brave man to accept the throne. While Milyukov, the inveterate liberal constitutionalist, begged Michael to accept in order to rally the masses to the traditional imperial flag, the socialist Kerensky warned the would-be Tsar that his life could not be guaranteed, a fact which Rodzyanko was bound to confirm. Michael therefore declined and the Provisional Government found itself nominally the supreme power.

The new government represented two clearly defined aims. First, it was the democratic successor to Tsarist absolutism and was, therefore, committed to convening a constituent assembly which should decide the country's future. This firmly held conviction determined the new government's view of itself as 'provisional', or 'temporary', a mere caretaker. And secondly, it represented the 'war party', the opposition platform which had been claiming it could conduct the war more effectively than the Tsar's government. In the course of 1917, the Provisional Government, in all its changing complexions, would discover that social revolution conducted simultaneously with war imposes intolerable strain, both on the country's resources and, equally important, on the national psychology. The Tsar's freedom of action had not been as great as the opposition had imagined. Only in November 1916, Milyukov had himself admitted, though for the wrong reasons, 'you cannot fight an external war with a war going on inside the country'. The truth of his words was no less when the old regime had been swept away and the new regime set itself the impossible task of rallying the people to a flag on which the colours were constantly changing.

9

The Socialists and the War

The official policy of all socialists on the question of war had been framed at the Socialist International Congress at Stuttgart in August 1907. Wars, it was stated, were only in the interest of the ruling classes and stemmed from the very nature of capitalism. They were created purposely in order to divert the workers from the class struggle, by confusing them with feelings of patriotism and nationalism. Socialist members of parliament, like the workers themselves, were enjoined to oppose armaments and to refuse the means for their manufacture. They must exert every effort to prevent the outbreak of war, in which course they would be supported by the 'consolidating activity' of the International Socialist Bureau. If despite all these efforts war should break out, socialists must intervene to bring it to a speedy end and at the same time use the 'economic and political crisis brought about by the war to rouse the peoples and thereby hasten the abolition of a capitalist rule'.[1]

The last clause had been inserted on the initiative of Lenin and Rosa Luxemburg. Since the subscribing parties were themselves divided over the issues of national and international interests, the 'official' policy had little binding influence nor could it be regarded as representative.

Seven years later the working classes and their leaders found their international solidarity put to the test. The workers behaved as they had been expected to do and, roused against the 'false enemy', they demonstrated their love and loyalty to their 'capitalist ruling classes', to whose defence they rushed. As for their leaders, very few resisted the tide and tried to put into effect the Stuttgart resolution. Otherwise the socialist members of parliament of all the belligerent powers, with two exceptions, voted to support their governments in national defence. Arguing that the survival of the socialist movement and the cause of labour would be threatened by defeat—whether at the hands of 'absolutist Russia', or of 'militarist Prussia'—socialists on both sides rationalised their surrender to what they regarded as the primitive and unconscious interest of the tribe.

The two exceptions were the Serbian and Russian Social Democrats. The Russian Social Democrat deputies in the Duma, Bolsheviks and Mensheviks, proclaimed their opposition to the war and on 8 August ostentatiously walked out of the Duma session, at which the rest of the deputies, apart from some of the Socialist Revolutionaries, voted for war credits. Their act was one of complete independence, performed purely on the basis of personal conviction and the policy of the Socialist International, and not in consultation with their faction and party leaders.

For the Social Democrats inside Russia the question whether to be faithful to one's internationalist principles or to defend the fatherland was soon rendered academic by administrative methods applied by the state. To oppose the war was to invite arrest and deportation—a fate which, before the end of 1914, had befallen all the Bolshevik deputies in the Duma. The underground organisations, which had been extremely reduced even before the war, were now rendered negligible by the police. A small group of non-factional Social Democrats, which had arisen in Petrograd in 1912 on the platform of party unity, did manage to survive in the rigorous circumstances imposed by the police. This Interdistrict Committee (*Mezhrayonka*), as it was known, held internationalist views on the war and tried to agitate the workers to turn the imperialist war into civil war. But open activity was out of the question: the workers were not receptive to these ideas, in the first year of the war at least. The Committee found plenty of excuses to delay bringing out its first anti-war news-sheet until December 1915, a time, it should be noted, when the temper of opposition and discontent was rising in general.

Many Social Democrat leaders spent the war in Siberian exile. Others either offered their services in the armed forces, in order to defend Russian socialist hopes from annihilation by German imperialism, or they entered the public organisations, when these came into being, there to await a more propitious time for revolutionary activity.

The abstract detachment of Russian socialists in European exile was shattered by the outbreak of war. Those who found themselves in belligerent countries were everywhere besieged by a great show of patriotic fervour, which sharply accentuated their self-imposed lack of a fatherland. Non-political Russian émigrés rushed to volunteer for the Allied armed forces and many political exiles found good reasons to join them. German militarism was a threat to French and English democracy, and its victory would also mean the end of German socialism. Among the 9,000 Russians who volunteered in Paris were the majority of the Social Democrats and Socialist Revolutionaries who were living there. Some eighty of them were recruited by a Bolshevik for service in the 'Russian Republican Detachment'. With consummate casuistry their manifesto, also composed by a Bolshevik, called upon Russian socialists to fight against German militarism as the last bulwark of Tsarist Russia. Under the French flag they proclaimed their slogans: for democracy, the German Republic, German socialism, and against Tsarism.[2]

Pressures of a different kind came to bear on those Russian socialists living at the outbreak of war in countries hostile to Russia, that is Germany and Austria. This category included a number of leaders, like Trotsky in Austria, and Lenin in Austrian Galicia. Alexandra Kollontai describes[3] the tribulations of Russians living in Berlin at that time. At the outbreak of war they were arrested, but were soon released when the authorities discovered that they hated their Tsar much more than they hated his enemies. Leading German Social Democrats proposed that the Russians should be sent home to raise a campaign against the war. The Social Democrat colony, some fifty-eight in number, protested that they would not be bribed with safety in order to do Kaiser Wilhelm's dirty work. Moreover the majority of the group had no intention of going back to Russia, but only wanted to get out of Germany into neutral territory, where they could carry on their internationalist opposition to the war. And this the Germans helped them to do.

On 8 August, the day the Social Democrats in the Duma demonstrated against the war, Lenin, who was living in Austrian Galicia, was arrested as a Russian spy. His quick release was secured by Victor Adler, leader of the Austrian Social Democrats now enjoying a certain influence thanks to their support of their government's war policy. Ironically, Adler was put onto the affair by a *Bundist*, Abramovich, and a non-factional ex-Menshevik, Ryazanov, both of whom held internationalist views on the war, but neither of whom approved of Lenin's party tactics. Social-Democratic blood on this occasion ran thicker than factional water.[4] Adler told the Austrian police that Lenin, if released, could be expected to run a powerful campaign against Tsarism and the Allies, and would thus be of greater service to the Central Powers at large, than he would be sitting in gaol.

After ten days Lenin, his wife, and her aged mother were all released and granted permission to travel to Switzerland, which they reached on 5 September. Thereafter Lenin was wholly engaged on the task of spreading and getting accepted his ideas on the nature of the war and its implications for the socialist revolution. He brought to the new situation a heightened fury against those who did not at once accept his views, but now his touchstone was less subtle, less hair-splitting than it had ever been. A war, he had indicated in 1913, would be a very useful thing for the revolution, though then he had been doubtful whether 'Franz Josef and Nikolasha [Nicolas II] will give us that satisfaction'.[5] Now that it had come he was determined to exploit it to the full. He had noted the strain which was imposed on society and state in the events of 1905. His amendment to the Socialist International's resolution on war, at Stuttgart in 1907, calling on socialists to use this crisis as a means to rouse the masses on to revolution, had been based on the experience of those events. In 1914 he converted this amendment into the simpler, more potent formula: we must turn the imperialist war into civil war.

Lenin was convinced that the defeat of Tsarism would be the 'very least' evil that could come from the war. To one of his best agents, Alexander Shlyapnikov, who kept him in touch with the remnant of the underground through the Scandinavian network, he wrote in October 1914 that one of their main tasks must be to combat the chauvinism generated by the war and the 'traitors' at the head of the Socialist International. The most effective way of achieving this first aim would be to spread defeatist propaganda. Lenin's policy was to convince the Russian masses, at home and at the front, that it was actually to their advantage that their fatherland should be defeated. By hammering home the traditional socialist message that nothing was worse than Tsarist absolutism, that it was indeed a hundred times worse than Kaiserism, he aimed at turning national war into civil war. The work must be carried out 'doggedly and systematically' and '*all* our propaganda and agitation must follow this line'.[6]

The idea of converting any section of the army to wage civil war, to turn their rifles on their own officers, was received by the other Social Democrats in Zurich as stupendously unreal. The 'internationalism' of the exiles in Switzerland was based on the demand for peace, immediately and without annexations, and without victors or vanquished. In practical terms their efforts were devoted to assembling the socialist leaders of all countries again in order to try to get a coordinated appeal to the people of the warring countries to stop fighting. Out of their attempts they hoped also to resurrect the Socialialist International.

The old factional issues were heavily overlaid by the intrusion of the new and unanswerable element of war, and in the main the reshuffle of alliances among the non-Leninist groups was according to the single issue, victory or peace. Hostility between the factions had never been extensive on the personal level, with the exception of Lenin and Plekhanov, neither of whom found it easy to talk to their ideological enemies. With the war there was still less personal rancour and ties were strengthened between Bolsheviks and Mensheviks, Polish Social Democrats and *Bundists*.

While Lenin had fumed in his Austrian gaol, his Bolshevik followers abroad had fidgeted in ignorance of the attitude they ought to adopt towards the war. As we have seen, many of them followed their instinct and joined the Allied armies. In Switzerland, Lenin now had to harden his followers into revolutionaries of the most extreme type, revolutionaries who remain subversive in time of major war.

Lenin was not alone in his militant stand against the war. In Switzerland, in particular, there were a number of socialists who dissented from the majority platform of their parties and were agitating for an early peace. In September 1915 they organised a conference at the Swiss village of Zimmerwald, where they composed an extremely militant manifesto appealing to the workers 'to reorganise and begin the struggle for peace'. The manifesto was signed by German, French, Italian, Rumanian, Bulgarian, Swedish, Norwegian, Dutch and Swiss Socialists. It was also signed by the Russians, Lenin, Akselrod (Menshevik) and Mark Natanson (Socialist Revolutionary). Three Polish Social Democrats signed, one of whom was Hanecki-Fürstenberg, a confidential agent of Lenin's. Trotsky was also there, as well as Martov, and a *Bundist* delegate. At this first Zimmerwald Conference, as it became known, a left group emerged, consisting of Lenin, his faithful aide Zinoviev, and the more independent Radek; the Swedes Nerman and Höglund; and the Lettish Bolshevik Berzin. Their aim was to give clearer directives to the workers as to the means of struggle, and specifically 'Civil war . . . between the classes—that is our slogan'.[7]

Lenin's Zimmerwald activities were concentrated mainly on rallying as much support as possible among the extremists of the left for his own Bolshevik platform. When a second conference met, at Kienthal, in April 1916 (known as the Second Zimmerwald Conference) the left influence was felt in the militant resolution of the majority, which now told the workers '*There is but one effective means of preventing future wars: the seizure of political power and the abolition of capitalist property by the working class. Lasting peace can only result from victorious socialism.*' The workers of the world were now enjoined to 'Rise up and fight' and to use 'every means at your disposal . . . to end quickly this slaughter!'.

Even this much militancy was not enough for Lenin who put forward a left resolution calling on the workers to ' . . . Lay down your weapons. You should turn them only against the common foe—the capitalist governments. . . .'[8]

To his extreme policy of defeatism and civil war Lenin added a no less explosive element: agitation on the basis of the party's nationalities policy. The Social Democratic position on the national question had for years been the indeterminate formula of 'self-determination'. This had been thought safe neutral ground on which internationally-minded socialists could stand without becoming involved in awkward issues. They satisfied themselves that nationalism was a product of capitalist relations and, like war, was used by the bourgeoisie and the ruling classes to dim the class-consciousness of the masses when necessary. The Jewish *Bund*, like the Austrian Social Democrats and Polish Socialists earlier, had already attempted at the turn of the century to formulate a solution to specific national needs, as distinct from the interests of the international proletarian brotherhood. The reaction was violent. Firstly, the large number of Jews in the Russian party had resented and feared the implications for their own international outlook, should the *Bund*'s claim to represent all the Jewish 'workers' in the Russian party be recognised. Secondly the party's centralistic tendency, which was Lenin's hallmark, militated strongly against any notion of building the party on anything but a unitary pattern. National, like regional, demarcation was regarded as divisive and destructive of unity.

The Mensheviks, who were supported by the various national parties, like the *Bund* and the Georgians, had yielded to the *Bund*'s insistence that more definite content be put into the party's national programme, and by 1912 they had accepted the formula of 'national cultural autonomy'. Lenin attacked this platform on the ground that it was not the business of Social Democrats to promote nationalist aspiration. The traditional formula of self-determination was, in his view, ample for the satisfaction of any conceivable national movement. For Lenin and most of the Russian party, as distinct from the national minority parties, national policy had been satisfactorily dealt with by Marx's peerless slogan 'Workers of all lands unite!'. The national question would be solved by the unification of the proletarians of all nationalities.

Cohesion of his own party and the principle of centralism were the chief motives behind Lenin's attack. But frequently he made fierce comments on Russian chauvinism, as the most obnoxious expression of nationalism. And to the end of his life he seems to have feared the potentiality of this destructive force, as he also feared physical violence. But he was prepared to use war, the apotheosis of violence, for his own purposes, and similarly he was ready to exploit the potent force of nationalism.

Thus, as part of his private war against the Tsarist empire, Lenin intensified agitation for the self-determination of all nationalities. It was not a departure from official doctrine, it was merely a carefully timed emphasis of it. When the Tsarist empire was making every effort to repel assaults from without, Lenin was seeking every means to raise the hostile forces latent within.

There was, however, considerable hostility to his ideas within Lenin's own party. Lenin's past record of zealous internationalism was seen to be in conflict with his new campaign for the self-determination of all nations, small or large, economically viable or destitute, advanced or backward. It was pointed out by a group of Bolsheviks, led by Bukharin and Pyatakov, that self-determination was envisaged only as a consequence of the socialist revolution. They described Lenin's call for immediate agitation for self-determination as utopian, since it was inconceivable under existing capitalist rule. And it would become an irrelevance when the socialist revolution triumphed, since the workers-in-power would not want to oppress the people of another nation, nor exploit them economically.

The argument was carried on in terms more appropriate to an international court of law than to an extreme revolutionary party.[9] Lenin left the following ambiguous testimonial of Bukharin: 'Bukharin is the most valuable and most weighty theoretician the party has . . . but it is extremely doubtful whether one can consider his theoretical views fully Marxist, for he is something of a pedant. . . .'[10] Bukharin's pedantry in 1915–16 consisted in his not seeing that Lenin was concerned with self-determination not as a principle but as a revolutionary weapon. Bukharin's views were shared by other leading revolutionaries, not all of whom could be accused of pedantry. Rosa Luxemburg, an internationalist à outrance, passionately denounced Lenin's attempt to divert the efforts of the international proletariat on to the smaller and less progressive demands of national independence. Her beliefs, however, owed much to her fiercely anti-Polish feelings and the contest between her Polish Social Democratic party and the more popular Polish Socialist party, which precisely agitated on an anti-Russian, independent-Poland platform.

In replying to his critics, Lenin, whose chief concern was revolutionary action and not definition of a programme, nonetheless was bound to reveal the nature of his thinking on this thorny subject. In spite of his vehement hatred of Russian nationalism, he frequently identified himself with its abominations. 'We, Great Russians [he was then addressing a Jew], have treated the [minority] peoples of Russia boorishly, we are capable only of oppressing alien nations. Russia must be cut off at Kiev, Odessa, Riga, Libava (Libau).'[11] In due course Lenin would introduce greater subtlety into these views, but for the moment his purpose was to raise an unambiguous call for the destruction of the Tsarist empire, by the wholesale collapse of support and morale in Russia. He claimed that it was a matter of indifference to Marxists as to who won the war. The destruction of French and English democracy by industrially advanced Germany he assessed rather positively. This was an attitude which, in others, he regarded as germanophile opportunism. He was content to let the capitalist–imperialist dogs eat each other while he led the workers into a position to seize power where the ruling dog was weakest.

It was Bukharin's thinking that was utopian. Lenin pointed out that there was nothing to guarantee the correct behaviour of a victorious socialist revolution and a triumphant proletariat. The sins of imperialism and oppression he could not lay exclusively on the heads of the bourgeoisie. He had never expressed much faith in the innate wisdom of the working class, and the behaviour of its leaders in the International at the outbreak of the war did little to build faith in that quarter.

While the left-wing 'purists' deplored Lenin's 'opportunism', and claimed that it contradicted his defeatist policy, his words found an echo in more sympathetic quarters. To the subject nations of the empire the advantage of a Russian defeat was self-evident. It was a truth equally well understood in the multi-national Austro–Hungarian empire. The German authorities, anxious to find ways to weaken the Russian war effort, needed little persuasion that one of these ways lay in the national aspirations of the minorities, and another in the defeatism preached by Lenin. The coincidence of these two paths made him an object of interest to Russia's enemies.

Lenin's programme was ambitious, and it was no doubt also this which provoked Bukharin to call it utopian. The evidence indicates that Lenin and his organisation had little means, in men or funds, to carry their propaganda into Russia and into the trenches. Tenuous contact with the exiguous Bolshevik forces inside Russia was maintained through the Scandinavian underground, where Alexander Shlyapnikov conducted impressive clandestine operations. Funds were plainly not flowing into Lenin's hands. A number of efforts were made, however, by various intermediaries to channel money from the Germans into the revolutionary network, in the hope that by this means revolutionary propaganda and agitation would be promoted.

During the war the German Foreign Ministry was interested in the possibility of promoting revolution in Russia in order to knock Russia out of the war, thus leaving Germany free to concentrate her attention on the western front. From the beginning of 1915 the German Foreign Ministry pursued this aim, spending large sums of money, which were mainly handled by Dr Alexander Israel Helphand, known also as Parvus.

A Russian Jew from Odessa, Helphand was a prominent figure in both the Russian and the German Social Democratic parties. He had always found the factional feuds in the Russian party distasteful and regarded himself as a non-factional. Once close to Trotsky, with whom he had been active in the Petrograd Soviet in 1905, and whose ideas he claimed to have influenced, he was without doubt a highly intelligent man, and among his gifts was that—unique in his milieu—of being able to make a lot of money. In the years before 1914 he had lived in Constantinople, where he combined involvement with political Zionism and the Young Turk Movement, with profitable ventures in commerce. Parvus had a bad reputation among his more upright comrades. He had a prodigious appetite for money, and his taste in cigars was evidently more discriminating than his taste in women. Together with his choice of associates, this created about him an aura of shady disrepute.[12]

At the beginning of the war he came to the German Foreign Ministry and laid before them his grand plan. He told them that the Russian revolutionaries sought the destruction of Tsarism and the dismemberment of the Russian empire as the only path to social revolution. He reminded them that their own aims would be furthered by revolution in Russia. Therefore their aims and those of the Russian revolutionaries coincided, and it was in their interest to finance the latter. As the most vociferous propagandist of Russian defeat and national self-determination of the minorities of the empire, Lenin was naturally the most eligible candidate for support. Lenin, moreover, already had at his disposal a clandestine route into Russia, through the politically explosive Finland.

The Germans were also tempted into financing the Bolsheviks by one Alexander Keskuela, an Estonian nationalist and ex-Bolshevik, who succeeded in convincing them that Lenin and his organisation were prepared to do business. Keskuela told the Germans that Lenin had conveyed to him the terms on which he would be willing to conclude peace with Germany in the event of a successful revolution. Keskuela demanded immediate financial help from the Germans, which they gave, in the belief that he was as good as his word. The nature of these relations ensured their secrecy and implied great trust by the Germans, who were dispensing large sums of money with no means of measuring the efficacy of their actions. Nor could they go beyond the first stage of contact, for fear of upsetting the grand strategy. Thus they did not know whether the money which was handed over to Parvus and Keskuela ever reached Bolshevik hands, or was even applied to the revolutionary cause.

Keskuela apparently did not have the degree of access to Lenin of which he boasted to the Germans. But he was able to penetrate the Bolshevik network into Russia, and through it to disseminate Bolshevik literature in larger quantities than the Bolsheviks could themselves. Whether Lenin liked it or not the Germans were using his apparatus, through their own agent, Keskuela, to out-Bolshevise the Bolsheviks, just as the Tsarist police had once done through Malinovsky.[13]

Lenin refused help from Parvus and even publicly attacked him for his pro-German propaganda. Furthermore he warned his agents to beware of Parvus's solicitations. Parvus's own apparatus included a substantial trading enterprise operating in northern Europe, out of Copenhagen. The war had interrupted the normal flow of goods between countries, though it had not made them any the less essential. The practices of economic warfare threatened the markets of neutrals as well as belligerents. In consequence, trade was carried on either illegally or on the basis of highly complicated and devious regulations designed to frustrate the enemy, to aid one's allies, and to accommodate the neutrals. Inside this labyrinth there were abundant opportunities for big profits for the shrewd and adventurous merchant.[14] Such a man was Parvus. The Germany money and his own vast profits Parvus applied, directly or indirectly, to furthering his most cherished goal—the destruction of the Tsarist regime.

The extent to which money raised in this way eventually came into revolutionary hands in Russia remains obscure. However, in September 1917, von Kühlmann, the German Foreign Minister, reported that the 'Bolshevik movement could never have attained the scale or the influence which it has today without our continual support'.[15]

If before the March Revolution the Germans were eager to finance Lenin's defeatist propaganda, they became doubly determined when it emerged that the new Provisional Government, with its clear intention to fight on, enjoyed wide popularity and support. The German authorities quickly recognised the value of smuggling into Russia, not defeatist literature, but its most persuasive author, Lenin. On his part, Lenin was equally anxious to return. Again the instigator was Parvus. Direct contact was unthinkable, both to Lenin and to his German sponsors. It would have aroused the immediate suspicion in Russia that his return was a special favour to the Germans, and his value to them, as well as to his own cause, would have been nullified.

The smokescreen behind which the Germans and Lenin at first sought to effect his return to Russia was unwittingly provided by Martov, the leading Menshevik internationalist in exile. Martov proposed to the Executive Committee of the Petrograd Soviet that it press the Provisional Government to negotiate the exchange of Russian Social Democrats for German prisoners-of-war. Lenin was overjoyed. 'Martov's plan is a good one: it *must* be supported, though *we* . . . can't do it openly. *We* would be suspected. Besides Martov, non-party Russians and Russian patriots should ask Swiss ministers . . . to *talk* about this with the German ambassador at Berne. We cannot take part directly or indirectly: that would only *spoil* everything. But the plan itself is *very* good, and *very* sound.'[16]

Lenin nonetheless remained in doubt about how to return. Various other routes were considered, through England or France. But the Allies would not entertain the idea of sending to Russia the man most intent on subverting Russia's war effort.

Lenin's intention to return under Martov's scheme, with the Mensheviks and non-party innocents, broke down, when the Mensheviks insisted that they would not move without the consent of the Soviet in Petrograd. Such a delicate operation as travelling through enemy territory into a situation where patriotic feeling was running high, demanded either a written guarantee of safe-conduct, or a readiness to gamble for the highest stakes. While the Mensheviks and the *Bundists* hung on in Switzerland for the Soviet's permission to travel home, Lenin and his closest associates accepted the risk of travelling under German auspices, with no guarantee of the reception they would receive in Petrograd. The risk, to Lenin, was far outweighed by his intense impatience to get back. To Inessa Armand, he wrote, in mid-March: 'In my opinion everyone should be thinking of only one thing now; to gallop [home]. But they're still waiting!!'[17] He would wait no longer. In April arrangements for his return were completed and on 9 April Lenin with some forty other Bolsheviks, including wives and children, boarded the famous 'sealed' train, for their journey through Germany to Sweden, and thence to Russia.

Seven days later they arrived at the Finland Station in Petrograd. There they were greeted by Menshevik leaders from the Soviet, who told Lenin that they expected him to join them in defending the achievements of the revolution. Ignoring them, Lenin turned to the waiting crowd of soldiers, sailors and workers and proclaimed that the German workers were about to turn their rifles on their capitalist exploiters. 'The Russian revolution, achieved by you, has opened a new epoch.'[18] At first it seemed he was saying that the Russian revolution had been accomplished and was the spearhead of world revolution. Perhaps he was making a placatory gesture lest his journey through enemy territory arouse animosity in the militant crowd. Later, however, when he confronted his own party leaders he made it plain that there could be no accommodation with this 'revolution'. Neither the Provisional Government nor the Soviet, as it was then composed, was enough.

As soon as he had heard of the fall of the Tsar and the emergence of the Provisional Government, Lenin had made his position clear to his followers: no change of line. In practical terms he intended to organise for the overthrow of the new regime and the establishment of a government of Soviets. The second part of this programme underwent radical revision on his return to Russia.

The overthrow of Tsarism had come to mean nothing. The Russian revolution of March 1917 was for Lenin a disappointing repetition of 'the old European pattern. The workers engage in bloody battles for a week and Milyukov + Guchkov + Kerensky are in power.'[19] The presence in Russia of a government publicly dedicated to democratic reforms and success in the war brought Lenin's maximalist programme into sharper relief. He knew that the new government would not be able to answer his challenge and at the same time retain control. He preached that the workers must not support a government that was incapable of providing the four staples for which the people starved: peace, bread, freedom, land. The issue of war alone had been enough to bring down Tsarism. Given the social disruption and emotional release which that event had provoked, the explosive potential of Lenin's issues would soon be put to the test.

1917

The overthrow of the monarchy and the emergence of a new government, issuing from the Duma, created an atmosphere of jubilation and release throughout the population. The prisons were opened and revolutionaries of long experience flocked back to the capitals. The spring of 1917 had at last made good the broken promises held out in the autumn of 1905. Led by the Kadets, the political heroes of 1905, the new government represented the victory of Russian liberalism after its long struggle for power.

Some Allied spokesmen in western Europe believed that the Russian revolution had been undertaken in order to serve the Allied cause. Indeed, even Lenin stated the belief that the revolution had been engineered by the British and French ambassadors to Russia. Remembering his own reliance on the German ambassador at Berne, his high regard for the power of diplomats is understandable.

The Provisional Government did not in any way seek to unburden itself of the obligations its members had undertaken when they had been leading the attack on the previous government. They would do everything in their power to carry the war to a victorious conclusion. Thus, four days after Nicolas II had abdicated, the new government announced, in its very first declaration, that 'the Government will sacredly observe the alliances which bind us to other powers and will unswervingly carry out the agreements entered into with the Allies'.[1] Shortly thereafter the new government was recognised by the Allies.

Once the new leaders had realised that they must perform their duties without the protective sanction of a monarch, they cloaked the whole question of the nature of the government with the promise of a Constituent Assembly. This was to be convoked 'within the shortest time possible on the basis of universal, direct, equal, and secret suffrage . . . .'[2]

Thus two major undertakings confronted the new leaders: to conduct the war effort more effectively than the Tsar and to prepare the country for elections to a Constituent Assembly. The old regime had vast experience of administration. The new leaders, however, while they had some experience in the field of public service (Guchkov more than most), depended on popularity and trust for the success of their administration. Since the burden of their anti-government agitation had been to convince the public that they were more capable than the Tsarist government, it was naturally expected of them that they should show how. As the very first occupants of a seat of power sought after by generations of oppositionists, they were afflicted by the myths of omnipotence, by an anxious desire to merit this trust. One result of this anxiety was that their period of office was littered with explanations, justifications, apologies, rationalisations, promises.

Dissension already existed. The new government, while consisting overwhelmingly of Kadets, included Alexander Kerensky, already well known as a defence lawyer in political cases, and as leader of the Socialist Revolutionary-Labour group in the Fourth Duma. Kerensky was now also a member of the Executive Committee of the Petrograd Soviet and at the same time an intimate of the chief figures in the new cabinet. His personal alliances crossed all party lines, a fact which quickly brought him into conflict with all of them. Kerensky's presence in the new government, as Minister of Justice, however close his personal relationships with the other members, was proof that the will of the Soviet, or the voice of socialism, had been heeded.

Kerensky's acceptance of a ministry was also symbolic of the Petrograd Soviet's recognition of the new regime. But his participation in the government put the Soviet in a difficult position. For it was the Soviet's intention to maintain a vigilant watch over the actions of the new leaders. On the other hand the popularity of the new government, and the fact that it was widely acclaimed as the agency that had overthrown Tsarism, compelled the leaders of the Soviet to find a place in it. The Ministry of Justice was offered to Kerensky who announced, upon acceptance: 'the new Provisional Government has taken up its duties by agreement with the Soviet of Workers' and Soldiers' Deputies'.[3]

From the outset of its existence the new government recognised the power of sanction which the Soviet could exercise over its actions. Its first acts were aimed at eliminating the worst excesses of the old regime, including capital punishment and political offences. These measures typified the government's liberal intentions, but also signalled its latent weakness in face of indiscipline.

The countryside was rife with anarchy. The peasants, in and out of uniform, seized the moment of general relaxation to square accounts. Soldiers wandering back from their units to the village brought with them the message of revolution, which they and the peasants understood as the signal to grab land and property. It was plain that if the new regime was to flourish and succeed in its two major undertakings, then its first task must be to restore order and the line of command. The government's chief difficulty arose from the national mood, from the fact that the peasants and the troops understood the overthrow of the monarchy as the signal for a free-for-all: abandonment of discipline, 'distribution' of the land. And since the credentials of the new government were franked with 'freedom', the mood of jubilation which greeted its emergence was in effect celebration of the advent of this ideal.

Disintegration of discipline in the army was accelerated at the

very beginning of the March revolution by the famous Order
No. 1, issued over the signature of the Soviet. In this, the troops
were enjoined to form their own soviets, thus bringing the
military under the supervision of the Petrograd Soviet; arms and
equipment were to be kept at the disposal of the soldiers' soviets,
and 'in no case should they be turned over to officers, even at their
demand'.[4] The 'dual power' was being extended to the armed
forces. But the Order made clear that during the performance
of their duties the troops must observe the strictest discipline.
In their private and political life, soldiers were to abandon the
customary signs of status. On duty, however, they should simply
address their officers as Mister General, etc. Conversely officers
must not be allowed to use the 'debasing' familiar form (thou)
when addressing men in the ranks.

The Order No. 1 was intended to establish democracy in the
army. It and subsequent, more excited 'orders', often not issued
by the Soviet but by some other unofficial body, succeeded
instead in spreading disruption in the ranks and demoralisation
among the officers.

The Soviet in Petrograd, like its counterparts which sprang up
all over Russia, was non-factional, in spirit as well as in name.
As a council of workers', soldiers' and peasants' representatives,
it was the symbol of socialist unity, where Socialist Revolutionaries and Social Democrats could shed their party interests
and act in the name of the masses. Although the soviets enjoyed
the backing of the army they did not regard themselves as
candidates for power. Instead they saw their role in safeguarding
the interests of the masses and in influencing the Provisional
Government, which they regarded as the organ of the victorious
bourgeoisie. Thus the government must be pressed to strive for a
democratic peace, a peace without annexations or reparations;
at the same time the majority of socialists, and the soviets as a
body, recognised the need for the war to continue on a defensive
basis. 'Revolutionary defencism' became the most popular slogan
of the socialists; the tender shoots of the democratic republic-

to-be must be defended from the onslaught of Prussian militarism.

Even the Bolshevik organisation in Petrograd went through the shift to 'revolutionary patriotism'. Until March, *Pravda*, the Bolshevik newspaper, had been under the 'Leninist' editorship of Molotov and Shlyapnikov, and though its appearance had been sporadic its line had remained firmly defeatist. In March Stalin and Kamenev returned from their Siberian exile.* Finding themselves the most prominent Bolsheviks in the capital, they took over *Pravda* and set about bringing the Bolshevik tune into harmony with the mood of the masses. The new line was that Russia was experiencing a bourgeois revolution, that socialist revolution and the proletariat's hour of triumph were still a long way off, and that the Soviet must be supported in its primary task of monitoring the government and pressing it towards democratic reforms and peace. *Pravda*'s new line was 'resolutely to support the Provisional Government in so far as it fights reaction or counter-revolution'. On the war the new line was no less anti-Leninist: as long as the Germans continued to attack, the Russians must stand at their posts answering 'bullet for bullet and shell for shell'.

The Bolshevik line in the capital accorded with that of the Mensheviks and Socialist Revolutionary internationalists. Virtual unity of tactics led to discussions on unity of forces and the old flames of a Social Democrat loyalty began to flicker once more. All of Lenin's work and the hopes of his German sponsors, too, were threatened by these developments.

Lenin's plan of action on the eve of his return to Russia was to work for the seizure of power by the soviets. This was to be achieved by winning over the support of the most deprived sections of the population and by creating underground cells in the army. The Provisional Government was to be systematically attacked and unmasked. His policy was to be 'an *armed lying-low*, an armed preparation of a *wider* basis for the *higher* stage'. As

* Stalin had been sent in 1913, Kamenev in December 1914, together with the other Social Democrat Duma deputies.

for the party, the main thing, Lenin wrote to Kollontai, 'is not to get tangled up with any idiotic attempts at "unification" . . . [but] to carry on the work of *our own* party in a consistently *international* spirit.'[6]

Immediately upon his return, Lenin formulated these ideas for the Bolsheviks in what became known as the *April Theses*. Bolsheviks were to spread defeatism and encourage fraternisation at the front. They must attack the Provisional Government in every way with the aim of replacing it with a republic of soviets. All private land must be confiscated. The Bolsheviks to distinguish themselves once and for all from the traitorous Social Democratic movement must call themselves the Communist Party and on that anti-Social Democratic basis a new International must be constructed.[7]

The Petrograd Bolsheviks were stunned. They were being told by their leader to turn the Soviet into a battering ram, and with it to demolish the Provisional Government. Lenin, they realised, was out of touch with realities. He had been in Switzerland throughout the war and even before refreshing himself from his journey home he was proclaiming his old line of 'No trust'. Their feelings were expressed by a former Bolshevik who denounced Lenin's views as 'the truths of outdated primitive anarchism'.[8]

Lenin's consistency, evinced from the moment of his return, pleased his German sponsors. The Political Section of the General Staff in Berlin received the following message: 'Lenin's entry into Russia successful. He is working exactly as we would wish. . . .'[9] Against the waverings of his comrades Lenin waged a fierce battle of words, at two successive Bolshevik conferences, held in late April and mid-May. He threw in the full weight of his personal authority and succeeded eventually in winning over his following. He was the leader who could remind the Bolsheviks that they constituted the vanguard of revolution. But he had nonetheless to recognise the isolation not only of himself within his own party, a situation tenuously modified by his authority, but also the isolation which his extreme tactics must force upon the party as a whole. If the Soviet, with its enormous popularity, was seeking to maintain a *modus vivendi* with the government, then too precipitous a line from the Bolsheviks could turn the Soviet into the government's ally. Lenin had, therefore, to modulate his policy according to the temper of the masses which followed the lead of the Menshevik–Socialist Revolutionary Soviet.

The tactics and views of all parties and groups were continually rendered obsolete by the rapidly changing relationships that beset Russia from the moment of the Tsar's abdication. The *vox populi* that had greeted the March Revolution proved to be composed of voices only momentarily in harmony. The Provisional Government soon clashed with its uneasy partner, the Soviet. The government's pledge to the Allies to carry on the war to victory contrasted with a Soviet appeal, issued in mid-March, 'to the peoples of the world', calling on them to oppose the annexationist aims of their governments and to take the problem of war and peace into their own hands. Almost in echo of Lenin's 'civil war' slogan, the Soviet called on the workers of the belligerent countries to follow the Russian example and 'throw off the yoke of your semi-autocratic order ... refuse to act as the weapon of seizure and assault in the hands of kings, landlords and bankers'.[10]

In the view of the Foreign Minister, Paul Milyukov, the overthrow of the Tsar in no way implied a repudiation of Russia's wartime diplomacy: '. . . there are no such things as the "Tsar's diplomacy" and "Provisional Government's diplomacy" . . . what exists is a mutual diplomacy of the Allies ... which we share. . . .'[11]

The government issued a statement of its war aims, in which national defence was listed as the first priority, and seizure and annexation of foreign territory were explicitly repudiated. The Soviet, however, pressed the government to get Allied acceptance of this repudiation. On 1 May the government, to appease the Soviet, handed to the Allies the above statement of war aims.

Milyukov, who all along opposed the dangerous policy of trying to please everybody, and for whom the chief object of the government lay in prosecuting the war, appended a note of explanation, which he hoped would reassure the Allies of Russia's loyalty and firm intent.

Published on 3 May, the Milyukov Note became the object of a storm of indignation. Armed troops mustered outside the government building and demanded Milyukov's resignation, proclaiming the slogan 'Peace without annexations or reparations'. The troops were calmed by their Commander, General Kornilov, but the fever of protest had meanwhile spread to the working-class districts. Demonstrations continued with the more extreme demand for the overthrow of the government. Only when the Executive Committee of the Soviet exercised its influence were the workers and soldiers pacified. General Kornilov resigned, despairing of the government's weakness in face of Soviet pressure, and conscious of the fact that public order in his own precinct had been restored only thanks to the Soviet. He was followed for the same reasons by the Minister of War, Guchkov, and in the middle of May Milyukov found an excuse to resign.

The Soviet's influence and power in public life had been demonstrated as a political reality, and the government saw no alternative but to invite its leaders to join in a coalition. The natural resistance of the Soviet leaders towards participation in a non-socialist government was overcome by growing pressure from within the Soviet, which Guchkov's resignation did much to reinforce. The government was visibly breaking up and democracy in Russia was being threatened with internal anarchy and destruction from abroad. Thus a coalition government came into being in the middle of May with ten Kadet and six socialist ministers. Kerensky was now Minister of War under the continued prime ministership of the Kadet Prince Lvov.

Almost at the same time as the government received this socialist influx, the socialist community in the capital underwent a marked change. A flood of European exiles arrived back in

Russia from Switzerland, by the same route as Lenin, and from
other parts of the world. Within a few days of each other, in the
middle of May, there turned up in Petrograd Martov and Akselrod, Ryazanov, Lunacharsky, Angelica Balabanova; Victor
Chernov, leader of the Socialist Revolutionaries (one of the new
coalition ministers); Trotsky, Bukharin and many others, totalling
some hundreds. The internationalism and Zimmerwaldism of
these returnees reddened the complexion of the capital's socialist
population.

The new coalition faced a situation fraught with dilemma. When
expressed as the policy of the government, 'revolutionary
defencism' emerged as little more than Milyukov's 'Allied
diplomacy', it meant simply continuing the war. The motives
of this policy were of little immediate concern to the masses,
particularly the troops. Official propaganda conveyed a confusing
picture of a government dedicated to a democratic peace, while
still exhorting the tired army to fight on. The government's own
doubts and insecurities about failing supplies in munitions, food
and clothing only caused it to raise the pitch of its propaganda.
    The government had to muster support and enthusiasm for a
military offensive, to be undertaken in mid-summer in accordance
with its commitments to the Allies. Again the difficulty was one
of propaganda: the government was anxious to repudiate any
suggestion of expansionist intent, and to emphasise the defensive
nature of its actions. On the other hand, the Galician campaign
was plainly an offensive, designed to relieve the western front,
where the Allies were still awaiting the effect of the American
entry into the war.
    Kerensky as Minister of War had the impossible task of
explaining to the front-line troops why they must remain at their
posts and not be allowed to go home to enjoy the benefits of the
revolution. He performed prodigious feats of oratory. In the
rear, at the front, from armoured cars or the back of a magnificent
white stallion, Kerensky ceaselessly harangued the troops, his
rhetoric and predilection for dramatic postures before vast

crowds becoming legendary.* Often criticised as a hysterical, self-centred actor playing to the gallery, he in fact had the gift of being able to command respect and in the summer of 1917 he was certainly responsible for mustering the support of the public and the army for the Galician offensive, no mean achievement in face of Russia's war-weariness.

But his success, like that of the offensive itself, was short-lived. Three years of continuous war and little prospect of out-right victory were coupled with ceaseless doubts roused by the overthrow of the Tsar. Defeatist propaganda disseminated both by the Bolsheviks and from the Austrian lines seriously under-mined the fighting spirit of the troops. Furthermore, it was beyond the courage or capacity of the government to send fresh troops to the front from the enormous garrison in the capital, for such a move would have been instantly interpreted as counter-revolutionary, a means of weakening the revolution, and the already delicate balance of the government would have been fatally endangered.

Both the Soviet and the government urged discipline and warned that the democratic future of Russia was being jeopardised by military and civilian anarchy. Their appeals, however, had to compete with the rising clamour for peace, bread, freedom and land, a formula, repeated like a hypnotic chant by Lenin to the troops, garrison and front-line, and to the idle workers, roaming the streets of the capital.

Despite Lenin's openly subversive agitation, it was not generally thought that the Bolsheviks were planning to seize power. The party was in every respect a minority. In the middle of June, at the First Congress of Soviets, Tseretelli, a Social Democrat minister, justified the coalition by pointing out that there was no party in Russia ready to govern alone. To the astonishment and

---

* Leonid Kanegisser, who in 1918 assassinated the Chief of the Petrograd Cheka, Uritsky, wrote a poem in June 1917 entitled 'The Inspection' in which the following lines occur:

... *Kerensky on a white steed before the troops. He lifts his tired eyelids and makes a speech. Silence. Oh, a voice to remember for eternity: Russia. Freedom. War. . . .*

mirth of the delegates, however, Lenin retorted 'Yes, there is!' The coalition parties, the Mensheviks and Socialist Revolutionaries, were represented at the congress by over 500 delegates, while the Bolsheviks had only 105 votes, and even with the support which they got from the Left Socialist Revolutionaries, the Menshevik Internationalists, and the non-factional Internationalists, they could not count on more than 200 votes. But mirth at Lenin's self-assurance was clouded by the knowledge that throughout his political life he had propounded the doctrine that a small compact group of professional revolutionaries could accomplish more than all the efforts of organised mass parties; in 1902 he had written 'give us an organisation of revolutionaries and we will overturn Russia'.[12] His claim to be prepared now to take power rang true.

The composition of the new Central Executive Committee of the Soviets, elected by the congress, reflected for the first time the balance of forces in the soviets which had sprung up all over Russia: 104 Mensheviks, 99 Socialist Revolutionaries, 35 Bolsheviks, and 18 others.[13] On 22 June it was learned that Lenin, in spite of Bolshevik weakness in the Committee, was calling a demonstration for the next day at which the slogans were to be 'Down with the capitalist ministers' and 'All power to the soviets'.

Though Lenin himself was unsure of the outcome of this demonstration, he was prevailed upon by the military organisations and armed following of his party. The Soviet leaders anticipated that this was Lenin's bid for power, hinted at by him at the congress. They voiced their opposition to his 'peaceful' demonstration and warned that it might lead to bloodshed. Factory deputies conducted vigorous propaganda against the demonstration, and Lenin eventually called it off. On 23 June *Pravda* appeared with a blank on its front page, where the intended call to the workers to demonstrate had been left out.

Although this was a victory for the Soviet, the Bolsheviks still posed a serious threat. Since March the rising rate of desertion, and the increasing indiscipline in the capital led to more and more arms being passed into civilian hands, most notably Bolshevik hands. Moreover, Bolshevik propaganda among the troops and sailors of the Baltic Fleet was gaining adherents, who brought their arms along with their allegiance. The government feared to disarm the Bolsheviks, and the latter told their followers under no circumstances to surrender their arms.

The Russian offensive in Galicia, which had begun on 1 July with great promise, had by mid-July largely spent itself, and the authorities were awaiting the German counter-offensive with apprehension. To add to the mounting tension, on 14 July the Kadet members of the coalition cabinet resigned because a government deputation to the Central Ukrainian Soviet (*Rada*), had concluded an agreement which in Kadet eyes destroyed the government's authority in the Ukraine, conceded the status of a national government to the *Rada*, and prejudged a cardinal nationality issue in flagrant disregard of the opinions of the projected Constituent Assembly.[14]

The show of Bolshevik strength which the Soviet had succeeded in forestalling in mid-June found its outlet a month later, on 16 and 17 July. Tension among the soldiers and sailors had been building up as a result partly of the government's renewed military offensive, partly of Bolshevik agitation, conducted particularly by the Bolshevik military organisations. Among the workers, strikes for economic benefits were unabated and now almost habitual, creating tension in the factory districts. The crisis in the government caused by the Kadets' resignation undid the valve. On 16 July thousands of workers, soldiers and sailors, poured out of the barracks and factories onto the streets of the capital, shouting Bolshevik slogans for the overthrow of the government and for the transfer of all power to the soviets.

The Bolshevik leaders had had heated debate as to the wisdom of attempting to lead this massive demonstration. Lenin's policy was to allow the pressure to build up but not to assume open responsibility for it, or attempt to lead it towards insurrection before he could be certain of success. At this time Lenin was not prepared to risk his own organisation, should the demonstration turn into an unsuccessful uprising. When it did occur he was at a safe distance in Finland. But it was precisely Bolshevik agitation and Bolshevik organisation which had brought the masses to this pitch. As in Moscow in 1905 the Bolsheviks now faced the dilemma of how to contain the enormous force at their disposal, and to avoid being charged with cowardice if they drew back.

During 16 July the Bolshevik leaders in the capital hesitated, waiting for the movement to assume its full proportions and for the government to show its hand. By that night it was evident to them that they were in danger of losing an opportunity to seize power. On 17 July Lenin returned to Petrograd. But the situation was confused, and Lenin was not sure how the mobs would react to an open order to insurrection.

The most militant elements of the mob, the soldiers and sailors, held open anti-Soviet views, seeing in the Menshevik–Socialist Revolutionary Soviet the mainstay of the regime which was continuing the war. Yet the chief slogan of the demonstrators was 'All power to the soviets'. Addressing the crowds from the balcony of Bolshevik headquarters, on 17 July, Lenin made it plain that they could only defend the gains of the revolution by opposing the present government, though he was careful to avoid open incitement to revolt. But by this time the Bolshevik Central Committee, in Lenin's absence the night before, had decided to back the demonstration as a bid for power. Some 20,000 armed sailors from Kronshtadt were brought to the capital under Lunacharsky's leadership, but in the general confusion and milling crowds which again filled the streets, none of this organised force could achieve anything, and the disturbances literally fizzled out from lack of purpose. The Soviet which had been threatened for not taking power was still intact, and without power, and the government, though shaken, was still in command.

On the evening of 19 July Lenin and Zinoviev left Petrograd and went into hiding nearby. Their flight was prompted by more than the failure of the uprising, though they and other Bolshevik leaders had indeed been charged with staging an armed uprising against the government.

Lenin's flight was connected with the government's plan to arrest him and some of his most intimate aides on charges of receiving funds from the Germans for the purpose of organising subversion in Russia. On 17 July, while the Tauride Palace was still surrounded by mutinous troops, the Minister of Justice, Pereverzev, panicked and issued a press statement to this effect. Lenin's chief agent, Hanecki-Fürstenberg, then *en route* to Russia with what was hoped by the Minister to be damning evidence, was tipped off. He turned back to Sweden, and Lenin went into hiding. Most of the Bolshevik leaders were arrested. The mood of the revolutionary masses turned overnight into anger against Lenin and his associates. They now saw the July disturbance as a Bolshevik provocation, a device to rock the government and help the Germans.

The relief which the Bolshevik set-back gave the Provisional Government was, however, offset by the continuing crisis caused by the military catastrophe that was developing in Galicia; by the resignation of the Kadet ministers; and by the government's reluctance to do anything that might isolate Russia from her western Allies. The problem of peace was no nearer solution merely because the government was now composed solely of socialists. Russia's socialist government now under the prime ministership of Kerensky (who was also War and Navy Minister), still regarded itself as no more than a caretaker, putting off solving Russia's problems until the convention of the Constituent Assembly. The government did not even appoint socialist replacements for the Kadet ministers, but continued talks with the Kadets until the coalition was restored on 6 August. The coalition remained tenuous and the resignation of the Kadets was an eloquent sign that the government had lost the confidence of a broad sector of public opinion.

Lenin, though isolated and defeated, turned again to the attack.

He now dropped the slogan 'All power to the soviets'; for the soviets in their present composition were compromised and impotent, and to continue to promote them as revolutionary organs would be to deceive the masses. The victory of the revolution, he claimed, could now, after the July days, be accomplished only by the independent seizure of power by the revolutionary proletariat—a term which in Lenin's vocabulary invariably signified the Bolsheviks. They would be supported by the 'poorest peasants or the semi-proletariat', terms which disguised the armed mobs upon whom Lenin had relied and would continue to rely.[15]

In the absence of its most prominent leaders, the Bolshevik party held its Sixth Congress in August, in Petrograd, unhampered by the government. The state of the party and its new tactics were explained to the delegates, some 260 of them, by Stalin. The feeling of solidarity had probably never been greater at any party congress. Over the question of whether Lenin and Zinoviev should heed the government's summons to appear on trial for treason, the congress voted unanimously for Bukharin's resolution which endorsed the leaders' refusal to appear, since they could not be sure of getting justice, and which roundly condemned the government and the Soviet for slander.[16]

The government's attention was, however, mainly directed towards its own fate, rather than that of its internal enemies. At the end of August, Kerensky convened in Moscow a national State Conference of all parties. His purpose was to rally as much support as possible in readiness for the long-awaited Constituent Assembly, which he had finally announced for 30 September. Instead of national unity, the State Conference exposed complete lack of agreement. On the one hand those, like General Kornilov, the Commander-in-Chief, wanted to restore the death penalty for desertion and mutiny, to crush sedition and indiscipline in the army, and to stamp out the Bolsheviks. On the other hand those, like the Soviet leaders Chkheidze, a Menshevik, reiterated the need for the government to pursue the democratic promise of the March Revolution—peace and democratic reform. While both these spokesmen agreed that the regime must succeed and that it would only succeed in consequence of greater discipline and order, they were in direct conflict over means.

In Kornilov's strong words the socialists recognised a rallying call for the dormant extreme right wing. To the socialists, strong government was synonymous with military dictatorship, the end of democratic institutions and of the parties. The majority of Kadets, the monarchists and the right wing, indeed, believed that democracy was already doomed in Russia, and they sought a leader who would act resolutely. Kornilov, the vigorous new Commander-in-Chief, became the object of these hopes.

The greater confidence which moderate and right-wing opinion had felt since the appointment of Kornilov on 31 July was directly responsible for the fact that the soviets became more susceptible to Bolshevik influence. The difficult middle road, upon which Kerensky and his government depended, was becoming discredited.

The opportunity for Kornilov to demand more decisive measures from the government came when Riga fell to the Germans on 3 September. As Commander-in-Chief he requested authority over all troops in the Petrograd district. He also asked for permission to despatch a cavalry corps to the capital, where, under martial law, it would defend the government against a rumoured repetition of the 'July days'. For Kerensky to have agreed, in the prevailing climate of extreme suspicion with which the revolutionary soldiers and the soviets viewed General Kornilov, would have been to throw the government upon the mercy of whichever of the two camps might emerge as victor. He ordered Kornilov to relinquish his post at once.

Instead the general moved troops towards the capital as an open challenge to Kerensky. But the attack petered out when railway workers refused to assist in the transport of Kornilov's men, and the soldiers themselves were repeatedly exposed, with increasing effect, to pro-government propaganda by revolutionary troops at strategic points along the route.

In the capital the threatened *coup* had produced panic. The

soviets rallied to the government's defence, the government
provided weapons to arm the workers, the Soviet persuaded the
Bolsheviks to join forces and throw in their considerable support
in an effort to uphold the government, and the Bolsheviks were
thus furnished with more weapons for their Red Guards. Lenin,
who was still in hiding in Finland, briefed his Central Committee: the Bolsheviks must help to defeat Kornilov but must not
forget their hostility to Kerensky and his regime. This was
merely a postponement of the seizure of power for which they
were preparing.[17]

In its eagerness to survive, the government overlooked the fact
that the arms being handed out would strengthen the Bolsheviks.
For the time being the Provisional Government lived through yet
another crisis and emerged in what appeared to be an even
closer bond with the soviets. But the soviets were themselves
changing in composition: the Bolsheviks were gaining strength
and by end of September held the majority in both the Petrograd
and Moscow Soviets. The Red Guards refused to give back their
weapons on the government's demand. Kerensky had saved his
regime by a means specifically designed for its destruction.

To show his solidarity with the left-wing parties and to appease
their growing impatience with his procrastination over peace, on
14 September, in disregard of constitutional procedure, Kerensky
proclaimed the Russian Republic. On 27 September, the Soviet
Executive Committee convened a Democratic Conference to
which socialist and liberal parties were invited.

But conciliation was a utopian ideal. The crucial part played by
the Bolsheviks in resistance to General Kornilov now gave Lenin
the opportunity to say, 'The majority of the people is behind us'.
He repudiated the Democratic Conference, 'which the Bolsheviks
would have been wiser to boycott', as 'merely the compromising
petty-bourgeois leadership'. Repeatedly he urged his followers
to go to the factories and the barracks, to the least privileged
workers and the soldiers who dreaded being sent to the front.
'Ten convinced soldiers or workers from backward factories are

worth *a thousand times more* than a *hundred* delegates fixed by [the Soviet leaders.] . . .'[18]

From his Finnish hiding place, Lenin watched impatiently while the Bolsheviks in Russia hesitated. The Soviets in Petrograd and Moscow were now in Bolshevik hands, the Mensheviks and Socialist Revolutionaries had failed to give the soldiers peace, the workers food or the peasants land. Therefore the Bolsheviks must seize power at once, and in the name of the Bolshevik-dominated soviets.

Lenin's revolutionary zeal was invariably more intense when he was detached from the events he was eager to control; moderation always followed on his returns to Russia. The Bolshevik Central Committee in Petrograd was less eager to make a bid for power than he was, and at the end of September, having discussed his proposals, in his absence, they resolved 'to take steps to see that no manifestations shall take place in barracks and factories'.[19] The dominant figures in the committee were by now Trotsky,* Stalin, Zinoviev, Kamenev, Bukharin and Rykov. Their attitude, 'Russia is not ripe for socialist revolution', was but an inversion of the recognition that the Bolsheviks were not yet ready to start it.

The Democratic Conference was followed by the formation of the third, and last, coalition Provisional Government, which consisted of ten socialists and six Kadets.[20] The parties of the Democratic Conference had agreed to establish a Provisional Council of the Russian Republic, or 'pre-parliament', which would express the views of the parties until the convention, now delayed, of the Constituent Assembly.

Deeply divided over the question of staging an armed uprising immediately, the Bolshevik leadership was equally at odds in deciding whether to take part in the pre-parliament. Those in favour, including Kamenev and Rykov, were also those who were reluctant about the uprising and seizure of power, while those who

* Together with the Interdistrict Committee, Trotsky had entered the Bolshevik party at its Sixth Congress.

advocated boycott, like Trotsky and Stalin, earned Lenin's praise for their consistently 'Bolshevik' line.[21]

In the event, when the pre-parliament opened on 20 October the Bolshevik delegates, except for Kamenev, walked out after Trotsky had declared: 'The revolution is in danger. . . . All power to the soviets, all land to the people. Long live the Constituent Assembly.' The Bolsheviks thereupon walked out, to cries of 'Go to your German trains!' and similar such abuse.[22]

The government was fast losing control over the deteriorating situation in the country at large. The Galician debacle had unleashed a flood of desertions; expropriation and violence in the countryside mounted rapidly; disruption of communications and transport hampered food supplies; the picture of Tsarist disorder which the Kadets had painted in 1916 now loomed to far greater proportions, and was accompanied by a chain reaction of rebellion and secession around the multinational periphery. No doubt recalling the grand strategy of Dr Helphand, the German Foreign Ministry was firmly convinced, at the end of September, that Russia 'could be expected to collapse as a result of any further, fairly powerful shock'.[23]

Lenin continued to exhort his followers to prepare for the seizure of power, attacking Kamenev and Zinoviev for their restraint and brushing aside all excuses for waiting—waiting for the next Congress of Soviets, which had been delayed, waiting for the Constituent Assembly, which it was plain, to him could not give the Bolsheviks a majority. Any restraint he castigated as a pitiful betrayal of the proletarian cause.

Trotsky's truculence at the new pre-parliament was echoed on 23 October in the Central Committee at a session which Lenin, back in Petrograd since the end of October, though still underground, attended in secret. At this meeting all the most prominent members of the committee heard Uritsky, who was closely involved with Trotsky in organising the armed uprising, report that there were no more than 40,000 rifles at their disposal and that that was not enough for a rising. But he urged that as long as the party continued its agitation for a rising it had better do something to bring it about. 'We must *resolve* upon some definite measures.'[24]

The meeting did indeed resolve that all party organisations must be alerted immediately to be ready for the rising. Only Kamenev and Zinoviev opposed this measure, against ten in favour. In an act of unique independence, Zinoviev united with Kamenev against Lenin. They published a separate statement in which they claimed that to stage an armed uprising at that moment would be to risk the fate of the party, and that of the Russian and the world revolutions. They exhorted the party to rely on its support in the soviets and to await the Constituent Assembly, where 'our chances in the elections are excellent . . . With proper tactics we could win a third, perhaps more, of the seats. . . .'[25]

Kamenev's and Zinoviev's emphasis on the importance of the soviets reflected opinion in the party at large. The masses were behind the soviets rather than the party. The realisation that the soviets still played a vital role prompted Trotsky to schedule the Second Congress of the Soviets as the occasion for the Bolsheviks' seizure of power.[26] In this respect he represented a link between the view of Zinoviev and Kamenev, in favour of seizing power through the soviets, and Lenin's outright policy of a Bolshevik seizure of power, without reference to the soviets.

Lenin reacted to what he called Kamenev's and Zinoviev's 'strike-breaking' with monumental fury. They had betrayed the plans of the party centre to the enemy, they had violated basic discipline, by seeking to countermand a directive ratified by a majority of the central committee. They had had the shamelessness to assert that the party had not been asked and that this decision to seize power should not be taken by only ten men. In Lenin's philosophy it was precisely by 'ten men' that such decisions should be made. He demanded that Kamenev and Zinoviev be expelled from the party, adding, 'It is not easy for me to write these words about once close comrades, but I believe it would be criminal to hesitate, for if a party of revolutionaries does not punish prominent strike-breakers, *it is doomed.*'[27]

Preparations for the seizure continued in spite of the dangers thrown up by this incident. Trotsky, as chief of the Bolshevik Military Revolutionary Committee, with the technical help of a number of master-conspirators, including Uritsky, Volodarsky and Podvoysky, concentrated on timing an armed insurrection to take place simultaneously with the forthcoming Second Congress of Soviets. The Bolsheviks' most potent propaganda, fed to the garrison troops by Trotsky, was provided by the government itself: a renewed military effort.

The Provisional Government, still shackled by its commitments to the Allies, was helpless against its internal enemies, and frustrated by the steady decomposition of the fighting services. The government, now in constant debate with the pre-parliament, had still to wrangle with the socialists over its foreign policy, and to allay the fear that the 'suppression of anarchy' was equal to the establishment of a dictatorship. While Lenin exhorted his followers to stop debating and do something, the same thing was being said by moderate and right-wing politicians in the pre-parliament.

On 3 November, in response to Trotsky's call, the Petrograd garrison declared full support for the Bolshevik Military Revolutionary Committee and promised to place its entire strength at the disposal of the Second Congress of Soviets due to open on 7 November.[28]

On 6 November, the Provisional Government took steps, at last, to curtail Bolshevik influence, and attempted to close down the Bolshevik newspaper offices. The Military Revolutionary Committee under Trotsky physically prevented the closure. This first overt act by the armed Bolshevik force, though small in scale, demonstrated the essential fact that military power in the capital now rested with the Bolsheviks and that they need no longer fear resistance from the government.

Lenin urged his comrades in the Central Committee that 'delay means death', 'everything now hangs on a thread'. He told them not to wait for the Congress of Soviets, due to open the next day, but to arrest the government that very night. History, he said, would not forgive them if they delayed, for what they were 'definitely' able to win today, they risked to lose tomorrow.[29]

The government appealed to the pre-parliament for support in the strong action which it proposed to take against the Bolsheviks. But instead of support Kerensky was reminded that he should end the war and give land to the peasants. These measures, he was told, would immediately sap the strength from the Bolshevik cause, for it was on these issues that Lenin fed. Theodore Dan, the Left Menshevik who put this to Kerensky, added that the Bolshevik masses did not want an armed insurrection. Like Zinoviev and Kamenev at the end of October, Dan did not realise that the question was not of masses but of Lenin's 'ten convinced men'.

During the night of 6–7 November Red Guards occupied strategic points and buildings in the city. The Winter Palace, where the Provisional Government was waiting for Kerensky, was surrounded by Bolshevik detachments, and Kerensky, instead of going there, escaped from Petrograd to raise armed support from outside. It remained only to occupy the Winter Palace and the act of seizure was formally complete by the afternoon of 7 November. Resistance from units loyal to the government was negligible, for the reason that the government acted far too late and with too little resolve to make use of them.

The November *coup* was not a repetition of the July days. Zinoviev later wrote that in July the Bolsheviks had far more people out on the streets. In November the revolutionary crowds were smaller, and indeed Lenin had no need of mobs. 'We acted . . . as a compact military force.'[30] The Bolsheviks occupied a few strategic points in the city, arrested the government, and announced through the Military Revolutionary Committee that the Provisional Government was deposed. State authority passed into the hands of the Military Revolutionary Committee, 'the organ of the Petrograd Soviet . . . acting in the name of the Petrograd proletariat and the garrison'.[31]

The news was broken to the Congress of Soviets by Trotsky, while Bolshevik troops looked on. The Mensheviks and Socialist

Revolutionaries at the Congress realised that all their activities in the pre-parliament, and indeed in the soviets, had now
been nullified. For eight months they had pushed the government
towards what they had hoped would be a more effective, more
stable position. Far from seeking power for themselves, and
having immersed their party identities in the soviets, they now
found themselves dispossessed of both influence over the government and control of the soviets. Now they fixed all hope on the
Constituent Assembly, which was to meet finally in January 1918.
It acquired the promise almost of a totem, and was expected to be
capable of coping with all the problems and difficulties which, in
1917, could only be debated without end.

The notion that the Bolshevik seizure of power was unexpected
and that the government was taken by surprise is groundless.
The realisation, after the event, that Lenin intended to hold
power alone, that he had seized it only *in the name* of the soviets,
may have shocked most socialists and frightened a number of his
own followers, but these were specious reactions. From the
moment of Lenin's return to Russia in April, especially in view
of the auspices under which he arrived, it was evident that he was
more than a mere opposition journalist. In July the government,
the Mensheviks and Socialist Revolutionaries, and the Petrograd
population were in little doubt that they had witnessed a mismanaged threat to the regime, mismanaged but no less a threat.
With the collapse of the Kornilov *putsch* and the arming of the
Bolsheviks there could no longer be any doubt of eventual conflict between the Provisional Government and Lenin. But
reluctance to use 'Tsarist' methods against any section of society,
whether left or right; the dread of being branded 'counter-
revolutionary'; the risk of precipitating an armed outbreak in the
rear, with war still a threat from outside, paralysed the government's will to prepare for the eventuality.

Many reasons can be advanced to explain why the Provisional
Government, in spite of its shift along the political spectrum
from March to November, was unable or unwilling to take

Russia out of the war. It was a step which would assuredly have removed a major part of the appeal of Lenin's programme. The government constantly referred to its duties and obligations to the Allies and to the democratic cause which seemed authenticated by the entry of Wilsonian America into the war in April 1917. But undoubtedly the chief consideration, the self-evident predicate of the post-Tsarist regime, was that Russia must preserve her will to win. It was clear that any government that involved Russia in a defeat—and a separate peace would have amounted to no less—would immediately be involved in civil war. Unlike his opponents, Lenin was prepared to take this risk.

Postscript

To seize power was one thing, but to retain the acquiescence of the people depended on Lenin's capacity to fulfil the promises he had made throughout 1917. First and most potent of these was *peace*, the promise to end the war and demobilise the army. The 'peace' he in fact achieved was the paper one signed at Brest Litovsk in March 1918, an agreement which so reduced Russia's territorial patrimony that even hardened internationalist Bolsheviks regarded it as shameful and humiliating. Lenin's party had already split on the principle of making peace with Germany. Some clung to their ideal of world revolution and called for a great revolutionary crusade to be conducted by Communist Russia against German imperialism, a crusade to which the German workers-in-uniform would allegedly rally without hesitation. Others yielded to the 'revolutionary defencism' of their socialist enemies and argued for cooperation with the Allies.

Lenin dismissed the first course as fantastic and suicidal, and the second as equally disastrous, for it meant continuing the war. His primary propaganda appeal had been to end the war and to his pragmatic mind unless that aim were achieved straight away his regime would not survive, humiliated or not. In the event his party rallied around him. External threat neutralised internal crisis, and the march of the German army into the Ukraine, and the physical dismemberment of the Russian state, accompanied by the emergence of independent Poland, Finland and the Baltic provinces, provided that threat.

Secondly Lenin had held out the promise of *bread*, that is regulated food supplies. The complete dislocation of Russia's supply system as a result of three years of war, together with reduced production was followed by the prolonged ravages of the civil war, the forcible collection of grain to feed the Red Army, terroristic supervision of food production, and famine.

The most important step Lenin took towards restoring the Russian standard of living was in March 1921 when he introduced his New Economic Policy (NEP). Repeated outbreaks of popular discontent against the hardships and against the Bolshevik government which seemed unable to remedy them, forced Lenin to seek respite in retreat. The NEP was intended to bring this about by allowing free enterprise and market trading to replace the war economy of the civil war period. At last the peasants were able to feel that they really were in possession of the land Lenin had urged them to seize in 1917.

In industry the Bolsheviks had very soon to relinquish their dream of workers' control, and instead Lenin sought efficiency in disciplinary methods of controlling the workers. Trained and skilled technicians and managers, though officially the class enemy, were brought back from limbo to reorganise industry, and the party, not the workers, saw to it that they did not step out of political line.

Trotsky applied the same principles in his brilliant organisation of the Red Army, in which former Tsarist officers were employed to correct the nonsense, in his eyes, of an army commanded by its own rank-and-file, the soviets.

All these important measures were a recognition of the hardheadedness and the efficiency of bourgeois, capitalist society, in which ability counted above 'class'. Yet Lenin's intention was to secure benefit and stability for the Communist regime which projected the eventual destruction of that society. While less practical, more idealistic Bolsheviks than Lenin may have been appalled at NEP, the measures were immediately successful in that they pacified the peasantry and in general neutralised the population. Lenin's repeated maxim that he would trade with the devil if it advanced his own cause was carried out fully in these policies; he bought time to stabilise his regime, and expertise to advance it.

But he had never pretended that he condoned his political enemies, however useful they might be in the meantime. Thus from the outset of his rule Lenin made it clear that the parties of the middle class and what he called the petty bourgeoisie—that is the Kadets, Socialist Revolutionaries and Mensheviks—were to be hounded out of existence.

As we have seen, Lenin had always been acutely suspicious of alliances, mixed organisations, coalitions. Thus the naive hope of some leading Bolsheviks after the seizure of power that the new government would be a coalition of socialist parties, controlled by the Bolsheviks, was quickly dashed by Lenin. (The Left Socialist Revolutionaries who were allied to the Bolsheviks after October 1917, and who were permitted to have commissars in the government, were a small splinter group, and their presence was tolerated for appearances.) Lenin's attitude explains the dispersal by armed force of the long-awaited Constituent Assembly which finally met on 18 January 1918. There, at the most democratically elected and representative body ever to be convened in Russia, the Bolsheviks were confronted with an alien majority which outdid even the hopeful calculations of Zinoviev in the previous October. The Bolsheviks had won less than one quarter of the seats, while the Socialist Revolutionaries (proper, not the Left Socialist Revolutionaries) held nearly three-fifths. No Bolshevik idealists now suggested that they should yield to the will of the majority, or even that they should form a socialist coalition.

Before October Lenin had claimed that the Bolsheviks were the only party capable of giving the people genuine freedom, as opposed to a fraudulent form of it offered by the parties of the Provisional Government. The suppression of opposition opinion which he began as soon as he gained power and the physical persecution of the other parties which ensued, revealed that his definition of freedom was idiosyncratic. In 1918 his old enemy, Rosa Luxemburg, languishing in a German prison while Lenin was terrorising Social Democrats in Russia, composed a remarkable essay on the Russian revolution, shortly before she was murdered. In it she declared: 'Freedom is always and exclusively freedom for the one who thinks differently.' It was an insight which acquired increasing significance in Russia first under Lenin, then under his successor.

Repressive methods became habitual to the regime and were invariably justified, like its retreats, as an expedient to deal with a temporary crisis. Crises were indeed temporary, but the means employed to deal with them engendered long-term consequences for the party, the regime, and the country. Lenin suppressed dissident opinion by suppressing the dissidents themselves. In March 1921 the momentum of this policy carried him in force against the hard core of the Bolshevik Baltic Fleet, who revolted against his application of proletarian democracy. The Kronshtadt rising was in the name of Bolshevik promises made in 1917. The sailors and soldiers of the garrison demanded socialist freedom, that is freedom for all the socialist parties, and an end to the party dictatorship. In practical terms they wanted elections to new genuinely representative soviets.

Lenin dealt with the physical threat by sending the Red Army across the ice to crush the insurgents. He dealt with the political threat by making it into something it was not, something utopian and impractical. 'Believe me', he urged an American journalist in March 1921, 'only two kinds of government are possible in Russia: tsarist or soviet. Some fools and traitors at Kronshtadt have been talking about a Constituent Assembly. But surely nobody with any common sense can even imagine a Constituent Assembly under the abnormal conditions in Russia today.'[1] But Lenin's omitting to say that the insurgents wanted new soviets, points straight to where he saw the greatest danger to his own monopoly.

Lenin's regime had demonstrated its incapacity to settle political conflict by any other means than physical violence. Insecure from the beginning in its tenure of power, the Bolshevik government lurched towards stability on the two crutches of political oppression and economic concession.

The consolidation of Lenin's regime also owed much to the party's capacity for overcoming its own internal stresses and strains. The extent to which the party remained united depended on its leaders' sense of urgency and their evaluation of the various threats to the regime they had helped into being. But even these innate qualities of self-preservation and party loyalty were not trusted by Lenin who, as the party's splitter *par excellence*, lived in dread of splits. As issue had followed issue and crisis had followed crisis, so dissent in the party had found expression in successive factional feuds, and by March 1921, when he introduced the most fundamental and difficult of all his retreats, the NEP, Lenin decided to outlaw all such factions. Politics in Russia, till then surviving solely within the Communist Party, was thus completely removed from the Russian experience. The consequences of that legislation are to be seen in the manner in which dissident groups within the party dealt with each other and were dealt with as traitorous after Lenin's death.

In March 1921 at its Tenth Congress the party voted overwhelmingly in favour of Lenin's resolution to abolish all factions, and to maintain a vigilant watch against the formation of any groups inside the party. Though passionate appeals were raised against this self-imposed ban on freedom of thought, in the end the comrades voted in favour, no doubt aware in themselves of the fear of split and inefficacy which Lenin expressed in his new measures.

The momentum of perpetual crisis as the basis for survival had carried Lenin through a full circle back to his habitual impatience with the views of others, now even of those on whose solidarity the security of the regime was supposed to rest. From the Economists of the 1890s, and the *Bund* when Lenin was forming his party, to the Mensheviks, Recallists, Liquidators, God-builders, Defencists, Social Chauvinists, Right and Left Bolsheviks—his entire adult life Lenin had had to deal with 'some idiots or other' who were threatening to 'ruin everything'.

In September 1917, in his meandering utopia of *State and Revolution*, Lenin had envisaged socialism as leading to the position where 'the need for violence against people in general, for subordination of one man to another, and of one section of the population to another, will vanish altogether since people will *become accustomed* to observing the elementary conditions of social life *without violence* and *without subordination*'.[2]

In December 1922, a year before his death, in a remarkable series of private notes addressed to the next congress, Lenin lamented: 'If it has got to the point where Ordzhonikidze* could go so far as to use physical violence ... then one can imagine the mess we've got ourselves into. ...'[3]

By the time of his death Lenin's regime had accustomed the Russian people precisely to violence and subordination, and the habit, once acquired, would outlive more than one generation.

*Lenin's chief commissar to the Georgian Bolsheviks.

References

Chapter 1 (pages 25–37)

1 See S. H. Baron, *Plekhanov, The Father of Russian Marxism* (London, 1963) for a valuable full-length study, the only one in English

2 See L. H. Haimson, *The Russian Marxists and the Origins of Bolshevism* (Harvard, 1955) for an account of Akselrod's early years and the development of his ideas

3 For a definitive study of this subject see R. Kindersley, *The First Russian Revisionists* (Oxford, 1962)

Chapter 2 (pages 38–50)

1 Yu Martov, *Zapiski Sotsial-Demokrata* (Berlin/Petersburg/ Moscow, 1922), p. 268

2 David Shub, *Lenin, A Biography* (New York, 1948), p. 27

3 *V. I. Lenin, What is to be Done?* translated by S. V. and Patricia Utechin; edited, with an introduction and notes by S. V. Utechin (Oxford, 1963)

4 L. H. Haimson, *op. cit.*, pp. 97–101

5 Richard Pipes, *Social Democracy and the St Petersburg Labor Movement 1885–1897* (Harvard, 1963), p. 65; for a detailed analysis of these organisational activities see Chapter 5

6 *Ibid.*, p. 85

Chapter 3 (pages 51–64)

1 The fullest collection is to be found in the 5th Russian edition of Lenin's works: *V. I. Lenin, Polnoe sobranie sochinenii: pyatoe izdanie.* All references to Lenin's works, unless otherwise indicated, are from this edition and will be shown as *Soch,*

followed by the volume number. An English translation of the 4th edition exists but is less complete

2   J. L. H. Keep, *The Rise of Social Democracy in Russia* (Oxford, 1963), pp. 109–10: one of the best accounts of the subjects up to 1907

3   This is according to Lenin's own count, *Soch*, 7, p. 435

4   *Vtoroy Syezd RSDRP, Protokoly* (Moscow, 1959), p. 203; my italics

5   *Ibid.*, p. 371

6   *Ibid.*, p. 378

7   B. D. Wolfe, *Three Who Made a Revolution* (New York, 1948), p. 244

8   The best account is by Boris Nicolaievsky, *Aseff: The Russian Judas*, translated by George Reavey (London, 1934)

9   For a full study of the Socialist Revolutionaries see O. H. Radkey, *The Agrarian Foes of Bolshevism* (New York, 1958) and *Sickle under the Hammer* (New York, 1963)

10   *Soch*, 7, p. 51

11   George Fischer, *Russian Liberalism* (Harvard, 1958), pp. 135–38

Chapter 4 (pages 65–86)

1   *Soch*, 8, p. 170

2   See Michael Futrell, *Northern Underground* (London, 1963) for an account of this episode

3   Boris Nicolaievsky, *Aseff: The Russian Judas*, p. 234

4   V. I. Gurko, *Features and Figures of the Past* (Stanford, 1939), p. 294

5   Sidney Harcave, *First Blood* (London, 1964), p. 65

6   Akademiya Nauk SSSR, *Nachalo Pervoy Russkoy Revolyutsii* (Moscow, 1955), pp. 28–31. A full English translation can be found in Sidney Harcave, *op. cit.*, pp. 285–89

7   D. Shipov, *Vospominaniya i Dumy o Perezhitom* (Moscow, 1918), p. 325

8   P. N. Milyukov, *Tri Popytki* (Paris, 1921), p. 11

9   I. Deutscher, *The Prophet Armed. Trotsky: 1879–1921* (London, 1954), pp. 128–29

Chapter 5 (pages 87–104)

1 David Shub, *Lenin, A Biography*, p. 368
2 J. L. H. Keep, *The Rise of Social Democracy in Russia*, chapter 6
3 *Soch*, 9, p. 6
4 Leonard Schapiro, *The Communist Party of the Soviet Union* (London, 1960), p. 62
5 B. D. Wolfe, *Three Who Made a Revolution*, p. 315
6 *Soch*, 12, p. 63
7 *Ibid.*, 47, pp. 103–6
8 *Ibid.*, 12, p. 65
9 *Ibid.*, 11, p. 336
10 *Ibid.*, 12, p. 83
11 Keep, *op. cit.*, p. 247
12 *Soch*, 12, pp. 179–80
13 Shub, *op. cit.*, p. 86
14 *Chetvertyi (Obyedinitelnyi) Syezd RSDRP, Protokoly* (Moscow, 1959), p. 528
15 Wolfe, *op. cit.*, chapter 13
16 Keep, *op. cit.*, p. 293

Chapter 6 (pages 105–122)

1 S. S. Oldenburg, *Tsarstvovanie Imperatora Nikolaya II*, vol. I, (Belgrade, 1939), p. 345
2 V. I. Gurko, *Features and Figures of the Past*, pp. 423–26
3 M. T. Florinsky, *Russia. A History and an Interpretation* (New York, 1953), vol. II, pp. 1190–91
4 D. Shipov, *Vospominaniya i Dumy o Perezhitom*, p. 444
5 P. N. Milyukov, *Vospominaniya*, vol. 1, p. 413
6 Florinsky, *op. cit.*, pp. 1197–98
7 Milyukov, *op. cit.*, p. 431
8 Grigory Aronson, *Rossiya Nakanune Revolyutsii* (New York, 1962); George Tokmakoff, 'Stolypin's Assassin' in *Slavic Review*, June 1965

Chapter 7 (pages 123–140)

1 Leonard Schapiro, *The Communist Party of the Soviet Union*, p. 101

2 David Shub, *Lenin, A Biography*, p. 102

3 *Ibid.*, pp. 105–6

4 *Soch*, 47, p. 251

5 O. H. Gankin and H. H. Fisher, *The Bolsheviks and the World War* (Stanford, 1940), p. 25

6 *Soch*, 48, pp. 226–28

7 Quoted in Michael Futrell, *Northern Underground*, p. 65

8 *Soch*, 17, p. 29

9 Schapiro, *op. cit.*, p. 118

10 Wolfe, *op. cit.*, pp. 527–28

11 First published in 1964 in *Soch*, 48, p. 293; original English

12 The letter was first published in 1962 in *Istoricheskii Arkiv*, No. 1. The present translation is from *Soch*, 48, p. 294

13 *Ibid.*, p. 305; original English

14 *Ibid.*, p. 316

Chapter 8 (pages 141–157)

1 For a history of Scandinavian–Russian revolutionary contact including contraband, see Futrell, *op. cit.*

2 *The Letters of the Tsar to the Tsaritsa. 1914–1917* (London, 1929), p. 77. The original correspondence, which was conducted in English, has never been published by the Soviet authorities in whose possession it remains. The present edition is a re-translation from the Russian

3 *Ibid.*, pp. 71–72

4 *Letters of the Tsaritsa to the Tsar 1914–1916* (London, 1923), p. 125. Publishing history as for note 2 above

5 *Ibid.*, p. 130

6 *Tsar to Tsaritsa*, p. 203

7 *Tsaritsa to Tsar*, pp. 393–94

8 *Tsar to Tsaritsa*, p. 256

9 *Tsaritsa to Tsar*, p. 250

10 M. T. Florinsky, *Russia. A History and an Interpretation*, Vol. II, p. 1371

11 From A. S. Rezanov, *Shturmovoy Signal P. N. Milyukova* (Paris, 1924)

12 N. Avdeev, *Revolyutsiya 1917 goda*, vol. 1 (Moscow, 1923), pp. 13–14

13 *Ibid.*, p. 35

Chapter 9 (pages 158–172)

1 O. H. Gankin and H. H. Fisher, *The Bolsheviks and the World War*, pp. 57–59

2 The best account is by B. D. Wolfe, 'War comes to Russia-in-Exile', in *Russian Review*, 1961, No. 4

3 A. Kollontai, 'Voina. Otryvki iz dnevnika 1914 g.' in *Zvezda*, 1924, No. 4

4 Abramovich, *In tsrei revoliutsies* (Yiddish) (New York), 1944, I, p. 372

5 *Soch*, 48, p. 155

6 *Ibid.*, 49, pp. 12–14

7 O. H. Gankin and H. H. Fisher, *op. cit.*, pp. 332–53

8 *Ibid.*, pp. 407–27

9 Texts are reproduced in English in Gankin and Fisher, *op. cit.*, pp. 219–39

10 *Soch*, 45, p. 345

11 Litvak, *Geklibene Shriftn* (Yiddish) (New York, 1945), p. 247

12 See Z. A. B. Zeman and W. B. Scharlau, *The Merchant of Revolution* (London, 1965) for a life of Parvus

13 The Keskuela episode is definitively dealt with in Michael Futrell, *Northern Underground*

14 For an account of this business see Futrell, *op. cit.*

15 Z. A. B. Zeman, *Germany and the Revolution in Russia, 1915–1918) Documents from the Archives of the German Foreign Ministry* (London, 1958), p. 70

16 *Soch*, 49, p. 406

17 *Ibid.*, p. 409

18 N. Sukhanov, *Zapiski o Revolyutsii* (1922), vol. III, p. 15

19 *Soch*, 49, p. 399

Chapter 10 (pages 173–196)

1 *The Russian Provisional Government: Documents (Prov. Govt. Docs.)*, selected and edited by Robert Paul Browder and Alexander F. Kerensky (Stanford, 1961), vol. I, p. 157

2 *The Russian Provisional Government: Documents (Prov. Govt. (Docs.)*, p. 158

3 S. Mstislavskii, *Pyat Dnei* (Berlin/Petersburg/Moscow, 1922). p. 63

4 *Prov. Govt. Docs., op. cit.*, II, p. 848

5 *Ibid.*, p. 868

6 *Soch*, 49, p. 402

7 *Ibid.*, 31, pp. 99–118

8 Sukhanov, *Zapiski o Revolyutsii*, vol. III, p. 40

9 Zeman, *Germany and the Revolution in Russia*, p. 51

10 Avdeev, *Revolyutsiya 1917*, pp. 188–89

11 *Prov. Govt. Docs., op. cit.*, III, p. 1272

12 *Soch*, 6, p. 127

13 O. H. Gankin and H. H. Fisher, *The Bolsheviks and the World War*, p. 12

14 *Prov. Govt. Docs.*, I, pp. 389ff.

15 *Soch*, 34, pp. 1–16

16 *Shestoy Syezd RSDRP (bolshevikov). Protokoly* (Moscow, 1958), pp. 30–36

17 *Soch*, 34, p. 120

18 *Ibid.*, pp. 239, 262, 255

19 *Protokoly tsentralnogo komiteta RSDRP (b) (Protokoly TsK)* (Moscow, 1958), p. 55

20 M. T. Florinsky, *Russia. A History and an Interpretation*, vol. II, p. 1442

21 *Soch*, 34, p. 262

22 *Prov. Govt. Docs.*, III, pp. 1930–31

23 Zeman, *Germany and the Revolution in Russia*, p. 51

24 *Protokoly TsK*, p. 85

25 *Ibid.*, pp. 88–89

26 Leonard Schapiro, *The Communist Party of the Soviet Union*, pp. 169–70

27 *Soch*, 34, pp. 424, 426
28 O. H. Gankin and H. H. Fisher, *op. cit.*, p. 79
29 *Soch*, 34, pp. 435–36
30 G. Zinoviev, *Iyulskie dni* (Moscow, 1919), p. 3
31 O. H. Gankin and H. H. Fisher, *op. cit.*, p. 100

Postscript (pages 197–202)
 1 *Soch*, 43, p. 129
 2 *Soch*, 33, p. 83
 3 *Soch*, 45, pp. 345, 358

Suggested further reading*

Baron, S. H., *Plekhanov, The Father of Russian Marxism.* London 1963

Chamberlin, William Henry, *The Russian Revolution 1917–1921.* 2 Vols. New York 1952

*Charques, Richard, *The Twilight of Imperial Russia.* London 1965

Dan, Theodore, *The Origins of Bolshevism.* Edited and translated from the Russian by Joel Carmichael, London 1964

Deutscher, I., *The Prophet Armed. Trotsky: 1879–1921.* London 1954

Fischer, George, *Russian Liberalism.* Harvard 1958

Florinsky, Michael T., *Russia: A History and an Interpretation.* 2 Vols. New York 1953

*Florinsky, Michael T., *The End of the Russian Empire.* New York 1961

Futrell, Michael, *Northern Underground.* London 1963

Gankin, O. H. and Fisher, H. H., *The Bolsheviks and the World War.* Stanford 1940

Gurko, V. I., *Features and Figures of the Past.* Stanford 1939

Haimson, L. H., *The Russian Marxists and the Origins of Bolshevism.* Harvard 1955

Harcave, Sidney, *First Blood.* London 1964

* An asterisk indicates paperback edition.

Keep, J. L. H., *The Rise of Social Democracy in Russia*. Oxford 1963

Kerensky, Alexander, *The Kerensky Memoirs: History and Russia's Turning Point*. London 1966

Laue, Theodore H. Von, *Sergei Witte and the Industrialization of Russia*. London 1963

The Letters of the Tsar to the Tsaritsa, 1914–1917. Translated by A. L. Hynes. Edited and annotated by C. E. Vulliamy. London 1929

The Letters of the Tsaritsa to the Tsar, 1914–1916. Edited by Bernard Pares. London 1923

*Luxemberg, Rosa, *The Russian Revolution* and *Leninism or Marxism?* Introduction by Bertram D. Wolfe. University of Michigan 1961

Pares, Bernard, *The Fall of the Russian Monarchy*. London 1939

Pipes, Richard, *Social Democracy and the St Petersburg Labor Movement, 1885–1897*. Harvard 1963

Possony, S. T., *Lenin. The Compulsive Revolutionary*. London 1966

Radkey, Oliver H., *The Agrarian Foes of Bolshevism*. New York 1958

Radkey, Oliver H., *Sickle under the Hammer*. New York 1963

*Russell, Bertrand, *The Practice and Theory of Bolshevism* (1920). London 1962

*Schapiro, Leonard, *The Communist Party of the Soviet Union*. London 1966

Schapiro, Leonard, *The Origin of the Communist Autocracy*. London 1966

*Seton-Watson, Hugh, *The Decline of Imperial Russia, 1855–1914*. London and New York 1952

*Shub, David, *Lenin: A Biography*. London 1966

Sukhanov, N. N., *The Russian Revolution, 1917. A Personal Record*. Edited, abridged and translated by Joel Carmichael. London 1955

* An asterisk indicates paperback edition.

*Trotsky, Leon, *My Life*. New York 1960
Utechin, S. V., and Patricia, *Lenin's 'What is to be Done?'*
 Oxford 1963
Walkin, Jacob, *The Rise of Democracy in Pre-revolutionary Russia*.
 London 1963
*Wolfe, B. D., *Three Who Made a Revolution*. London 1966

* An asterisk indicates paperback edition.

Index